Your Education Research Project Companion

Your Education Research Project Companion

Second edition

Jim McGrath and
Anthony Coles

Routledge
Taylor & Francis Group

LONDON AND NEW YORK

First published 2010 by Pearson Education Limited
Second edition published 2013

Published 2013 by Routledge
2 Park Square, Milton Park, Abingdon, Oxon OX14 4RN
711 Third Avenue, New York, NY 10017, USA

Routledge is an imprint of the Taylor & Francis Group, an informa business

ISBN 13: 978–0–273–77479–2 (pbk)

British Library Cataloguing-in-Publication Data
A catalogue record for the print edition is available from the British Library

Library of Congress Cataloging-in-Publication Data
McGrath, Jim.
   Your education research project companion / Jim McGrath and Anthony Coles. – Second edition
      pages cm.
   ISBN 978-0-273-77479-2
   1. Education leadership – Handbooks, manuals, etc. 2. School management and organization –
Handbooks, manuals, etc. 3. School administrators – Handbooks, manuals, etc. I. Coles, Anthony. II. Title.
   LB2805.M334 2013
   371.2'011–dc23

Print edition typeset in 10/15pt Arial Light by 30

For Eija, Helen and Michael and in memory of my brother
Tony McGrath

For Jane, Bea and William

Brief contents

Contents

Tutorial 3

Writing your literature review

Tutorial 4

Choosing your research methodology

Tutorial 5

Tutorial 6

Tutorial 9

Tutorial 10

Companion Website

For open-access **student resources** specifically written
to complement this textbook and support your learning,
please visit **www.routledge.com/9780273774792**

About the authors

Jim McGrath recently retired from teaching to become a full-time writer. However, as a visiting lecturer he continues to teach on a number of MA modules. As someone who gained all his qualifications by part-time study, Jim is passionate about supporting part-time students to achieve their goals.

Anthony Coles is Reader in Post-compulsory Education and MA Education Course Director at Birmingham City University. Much of his teaching involves research skills and supporting teachers in their professional development. Anthony is particularly interested in supporting students to overcome any fears they may have about the use of quantitative methods in education research.

Other books by Jim McGrath and Anthony Coles:
Your Teacher Training Handbook (2011)
Your Education Leadership Handbook (2012)

Also by Jim McGrath and Bob Bates:
The Little Book of Big Management Theories . . . and How to Use Them (2013)

Introduction

A book for first-time researchers

There are many good books available that deal with educational research. So why do we need another one? We believe that there is a need for a new kind of research textbook. One that minimises the use of jargon, provides user-friendly guidance on how to design and carry out a small-scale piece of research and recognises that many first-time researchers find the process of research stressful. Our philosophy is simple. We believe that if you know and can apply the principles that underpin research, you will be able to complete your research assignment and understand the myriad of other research books that are on the market.

Between us we have nearly 40 years' experience of supervising undergraduate and postgraduate students' research projects, dissertations and theses. We are aware that many students find undertaking their first piece of research a frightening experience. After all, isn't research only carried out by academics and scientists? Nothing could be further from the truth. We all do research every day, but we don't call it that. For example, when you buy a new car don't you read up on the various models available, visit a few car showrooms and speak to someone who already owns the model of car that you are thinking of buying? That is research. You are discovering information about an issue that is of importance to you.

So what is it about research that frightens people? We think that there are two main problems. Firstly, students think that research has to be 'original' and that they have to 'discover new knowledge'. The truth is much more mundane. At undergraduate and Master's level you can research a topic that people have been looking at for years – e.g. classroom management, the motivation of students or mentoring of trainee teachers – and still achieve a very good pass. So if a topic has already been researched to death what is the point of researching it again? It is valuable because what you discover will be new knowledge to you and it will inform your thinking and professional practice. You will also have learnt valuable new skills. Secondly, the language of research, the jargon used, frightens people – e.g. research methodology, triangulation, reliability, sampling sets and validity. No wonder people find it difficult to relate research to what they do in the classroom or office.

The sole aim of this book is to simplify the research process. We aim to tell you everything you need to know to carry out successfully a small-scale piece of empirical research. That is research, which involves collecting data from sources other than just books. The book will also be useful for students undertaking 'conceptually based research' where the researcher is solely concerned with using secondary data, especially Tutorials 1, 2, 3, 8, 9 and 10.

We explain the major stages in the research process from initial idea to finished assignment in a clear and unambiguous manner. We simplify the issues so that you can get a firm grip on the key ideas, but the work is not simplistic. Einstein said that great art was the expression of complex ideas in the simplest possible form. It is this kind of user-friendly simplicity that we seek. In addition we address the type of concerns and fears that new researchers may have at each stage of the process.

Format and style of book

The book is written from the viewpoint of Samantha (Sam), a PGCE student. This means that the process of research is examined through the eyes of the student and not those of an academic dispensing words of wisdom. We believe that this approach helps us to simplify and make transparent the research process. Sam is an amalgam of the hundreds of undergraduate and postgraduate students that we have had the pleasure to work with over the years.

Each chapter is based on a single tutorial meeting and deals with one aspect of the research process. The topics covered are those that you would find in any research programme. To avoid a purely theoretical discussion, examples of how to choose and apply research methodologies and tools are provided in the context of Sam's own research interests. It is essential that, as you read, you constantly ask yourself 'how is this relevant to my research and how could I apply it in practice?' Within each chapter, you will find:

- extracts from Sam's reflective journal;
- a transcript of the tutorial meeting between Sam and Dr Richard Reed, research supervisor, which Sam has annotated showing linkages to where further discussion on selected topics can be found;

- a summary of key learning points arising from the tutorial and agreed action points;
- a diagrammatical overview of the tutorial summarising the issues discussed and showing their interrelationships;
- handouts provided by Dr Reed during the tutorial.

Within each tutorial Richard suggests further reading that Sam may wish to undertake. Full details of Richard's recommendation can be found at the back of the book under the heading 'Recommended reading list and bibliography'. It is essential that you do not rely on one or two research books when completing your project or dissertation and we would urge you to dip into a selection of these texts as required.

Traditionally PGCEs were run at Level 6 (equivalent to the final year of an undergraduate degree course). Recently some universities have offered PGCEs at Master's level only (Level 7), while other universities have run the core programme at Level 6 and allowed students to take one or two modules at either Level 6 or 7. Sam's programme is at Level 6 but she can elect to take her *Research in professional practice project* at either Level 6 or 7. Sam is unsure what to do. Before she makes a final decision she wants to know what additional work is involved if she decides to study at Master's level. So towards the end of each tutorial she asks her supervisor to explain what additional work would be required if she was to complete the module at Master's level.

In addition to the above, a list of contents is provided at the start of each tutorial together with a short statement outlining the aims of the tutorial. However, the order of the contents is indicative only. This is because the nature of a tutorial means that the discussion may return to the same topic more than once and Sam's reflections are inevitably retrospective.

A glossary of key terms is provided at the end of the book which you may wish to refer to for clarification. Each key term has been **highlighted** in the text when first used.

As the size of this book is limited, additional materials can be found at **www. routledge.com/9780273774792;**   these   include examples of data collection tools, a series of checklists that can be used at each stage of the research process and copies of completed research projects and a dissertation. Best of all the entire site is free, so there is no excuse not to log on.

Summary content of book

Tutorial 1 provides an overview of the research process at Levels 6 and 7 and suggests how to tackle the problem of drafting usable research questions. Tutorial 2 explains how to structure a research report or dissertation. Tutorial 3 considers the notion of a conceptual framework, a concept that is particularly important at Level 7. It also provides advice on how to find and evaluate relevant literature and write up that all-important literature review. It makes the important point that you should always use a range of books and not become over reliant on one or two texts. This point is relevant to both your choice of texts in the literature review and those that you use to support your research approach.

Tutorial 4 discusses two popular research methodologies, namely quantitative and qualitative. Both methodologies are defined and their strengths and weaknesses discussed. Additionally, aspects of methodology such as ethics, triangulation, validity and reliability are introduced. Tutorial 5 reviews three popular research strategies: namely, case study, action research and survey. Each is defined and evaluated and guidance given on how to select the most appropriate strategy.

Tutorials 6 and 7 look at four popular data collection tools: namely, questionnaires, interviews, observations and documentation. An example of each is provided and guidance given on how to select the most appropriate method for your research.

Tutorial 8 examines how to analyse, evaluate and report qualitative data. A step-by-step approach guides you through the process of comparing and contrasting data, including making links with the literature review. Tutorial 9 considers how to analyse, evaluate and report quantitative data.

Tutorial 10 provides guidance on how to write up your research and improve your final mark. It also considers such thorny issues as how much is enough analysis and how you decide which data to relegate to an appendix.

How to use this book

Most people undertaking a research project or dissertation attend a series of taught sessions where they learn about the 'nuts and bolts' of the research process. On completion, they are allocated a supervisor who acts as their guide through the research process. For the purpose of this book, we have combined the roles of teacher and supervisor. Therefore, when Sam turns up for a tutorial Dr Reed provides a mixture of taught input and supervision. We realise that this is unusual but it enables us to discuss the full range of research issues faced by new researchers from the student's perspective. We would encourage you to think of this book as an addition to your research notes. So don't be afraid to annotate it and make it your own.

So how might you use the book? Assuming that your course has a taught research programme you may wish to:

- Read the relevant chapter or chapters before attending a taught session on the same issues. This will familiarise you with the key concepts and enable you to clarify anything that you are unsure of with your lecturer.

- Read the appropriate chapter after a session. This will reinforce the learning that has already taken place and provide a different perspective on the issues discussed.

- Use the summary of each tutorial's main points as the basis for your own notes and/or for quick revision.

- Study the overview diagram in each tutorial to identify and understand the interconnectedness of the research process. Visual learners may wish to study the diagram before reading the relevant tutorial in order to obtain an overview of the issues discussed.

- Use Sam's action points to guide you in what you need to do at each stage of the research process.

- Use the book as your primary learning resource when you have missed a session entirely, or found a lesson particularly difficult.

- Follow up the further reading recommendations provided at the end of each chapter.

If you don't have access to taught research sessions than you can use this book as your primary teaching aid and supplement it by using one or more of the suggestions made by Richard. When following up a reference, you should decide how much of the recommended text you need to read (some, most, all) and develop the habit of using the book's index to find key terms and ideas.

Occasionally, in the text, you will find a reference dated 20XX. This is a fictitious reference used solely by Dr Reed for illustrative purposes.

As the book also mentions some of the practical and emotional problems encountered by novice researchers, you can also use it as a source of comfort and impartial advice. On a wet, dark night when you are convinced that what you have written is utter rubbish it's comforting to know that every researcher goes through this stage, even those of us who have been doing it for a very long time.

Health warning

This book promotes a widely used approach to conducting and reporting empirical research; however, it is essential that you familiarise yourself with the requirements of your own institution, particularly in relation to the specific assessment criteria and ethical requirements relating to your assignment. This is essential as there are variations in custom and practice across different institutions, which, if not observed, could result in a reduced mark for your work.

We wish you the very best of luck with your research and if you have any suggestions for how we could make this book more useful to the novice researcher, please contact us.

Jim McGrath
Anthony Coles
Birmingham City University, 2013

Acknowledgements

We would like to thank our editors at Pearson, Rob Cottee and Catherine Yates, for their continued support and encouragement at every stage of the writing process. It has been much appreciated.

We would also like to thank Tracey Granger for permission to publish her interesting BA (Hons) Education Studies Dissertation on child safety on the website that accompanies this book and also Michael McGrath and Phil Taylor for their contributions.

GETTING STARTED

Aim of tutorial

To provide you with an overview of the research process and guidance on how to define the focus of your research and draft suitable research questions.

Areas covered in this tutorial

Note: Key terms have been **highlighted** in the text when first used. A definition of each term is provided in the glossary at the end of the book.

Sam's reflection

13 September, lunchtime

Dr Sue Storm the Course Director reminded us last week that we need to keep a **reflective journal** as part of our coursework for a minimum of three months. Needless to say I'd forgotten all about it. As if the PGCE wasn't hard enough without additional work. Luckily, I start my tutorials on the 15th with Dr Reed, so I can base my journal around my Research Project Module. That should give me enough information to reflect upon.

I've not had much to do with Dr Reed so far. I wonder what he's like. I hope he's not one of those academics that try to overcomplicate things.

Barry Allan was telling me that when he did this module he found it really difficult to take notes and listen to what his supervisor was saying at the same time. He ended up recording each session. I think I'll do that. It means I can concentrate on what's said and not worry about missing anything. I'd better give the good Doctor a ring and see if he is happy with me recording his tutorials.

Dr Reed sounded friendly enough when I phoned him. He asked if I was free to pop round and see him tonight for an informal chat. He's in Room FF4 the Baxter Building.

13 September, evening

Well that wasn't as bad as I thought it would be. Dr Reed, or Richard as I now call him, seemed really friendly. He wanted to know all about me. What modules I had previously studied. What my professional interests are. Where my placement is. He said that this background information helped him understand each student as a person. Of course he could just be nosey.

Funnily enough while he was trying to find out about me I was checking him out. Judging by the poster over his desk he's a West Brom fan.

Poor soul. One of my first boyfriends was a football fan and if his team lost I always knew we were in for a misery-filled Saturday night. Richard also had a mini library in his room. I wonder if he's read every book or if they are there just for show?

He asked me if I was going to take the module at Level 6 or Master's level. I told him I hadn't decided yet and he said that was fine. He was happy to spend a bit of time at the end of each tutorial talking about the difference between working at Level 6 and Level 7 – Master's level and he gave me a hand-out detailing the level descriptors (see Handout 1.1). He said Level 6 is equivalent to the last year of study on an undergraduate course and that Level 7, Master's, was a step up from that. But he didn't think that it was a huge step up. He believed that any undergraduate who was willing to work hard could handle Master's-level work.

Fortunately he was happy for me to record the tutorial. In fact, I think he was quite impressed with the idea. Apparently, some students turn up without even a pen to take notes. How can they hope to remember what a tutor says over the course of 45 minutes without some notes? So first things first. Richard asked me to jot down some ideas about what I wanted to research before I see him on the 15th. That shouldn't take long.

Review of tutorial

Recommended reading

Richard was reading his emails when I entered. He looked up and smiled. 'So our meeting didn't put you off then?'

'No, but tonight might,' I said with more feeling than I had intended.

'Grab a seat', he said and waited for me to get organised. 'Before we get started I thought it would be useful if I gave you a list of books and articles that I'll be referring to and which you might want to dip into (➡ *Recommended reading list and bibliography on pages 239–41*). I suggest that you use *Your Education Research Project Companion* as your core book. But it's essential that you back that up with some additional reading. So select at least one other book from the Highly recommended section and use it to clarify and sometimes challenge what is said in the *Companion*. As for the texts in the Recommended section, use them when you want additional information about a specific aspect of research such as questionnaires or interviews.'

'There seems a lot here. Do I have to read them all?'

'No. What you have to learn to do is use both the table of contents and the index to find what you want. How much you need to read will depend entirely on what's required for your research. Based on that you must decide if you need to read a paragraph, a page, a chapter or the whole book. OK?'

'Yes. What should I read to support this Tutorial?' I asked, keen to make a good start.

'From the recommended list I'd dip into McGrath and Coles (2011), Wilson (2009a) and McMillan and Weyers (2010). But I stress again, you should read just the bits that are relevant to you.'

Even dipping in to this seemed like a lot of reading but I just said, 'That's fine.'

Finding a focus for my research

'Good. When I spoke to you I asked you to identify a topic or issue that you wanted to find out more about. What have you come up with?'

'Well, I thought that I would look at teaching methods.'

'That's a good topic. What age group do you currently teach?'

'Eleven to 14.'

'OK. So why teaching methods?'

'My placement has been doing some work in this area. They had an OfSTED report that said some teachers relied too heavily on a limited range of teaching methods.'

'Fine. I always like it when a student can do a piece of research that they are interested in and which is of value to their employers. It means you can legitimately do some of your research during working hours and you are likely to get support from your line manager and colleagues. Have you thought about the **focus** for your research?'

'I'm sorry?' I said, unsure what he meant.

'What I mean is: which aspect or aspects of teaching methods do you want to look at? For example, are you interested in the difference between teacher-centred and learner-centred methods or do you want to explore how to use more student-centred methods in your teaching?'

'I'm not sure. I suppose I want to identify what methods are available, when I should use one method rather than another and which methods are most effective.'

'Good, you may not realise it but you have clearly thought about the scope of your research. Effectively you're doing an **empirical** study into the teaching methods that can be used in a secondary school, how to choose between the methods available and identify which are most effective in your school. Correct?'

'Well, when you say it like that it sounds as if I know what I'm doing.'

Formatting my research questions

Richard smiled. 'OK you have your **research focus**. Now you have to identify your **research questions**.'

'You mean like, "What are the best teaching methods to use when working with 11- to 14-year-olds?"'

'Not quite. Your question sounds like it has a specific answer.'

'It's supposed to have a specific answer isn't it?' I said defensively. 'It's a question.'

'Ahh! Now there is the problem,' Richard said. 'A research question can end with a question mark but it doesn't have to. The use of a question mark implies that there is a single answer and that you intend to find it. For example, your question implies that there is a "best way" to teach a group of learners, when in reality you will probably need to vary the methods you use with each group.'

'Because each group is different and what works with one won't work with another,' I said.

'Indeed. You'd be much safer saying, "I wish to explore which teaching methods can be used when teaching a group of learners in a secondary school".

This is an open-ended question and allows you to explore the various issues that are at play. By phrasing your question in this way you don't have to prove that the method or methods you have identified are the best. Proving something is virtually impossible in educational research, especially a small-scale piece of research like yours.'

Cause and effect in education research

'But, surely, if I used x teaching method and the learners' exam results improved, I could say that it was because of the new teaching method I'd used.'

'If only wishing made it so. There are too many variables at play for you to make any claims regarding cause and effect.'

'What do you mean?'

'There are all sorts of reasons why a particular method might have worked and it's extremely difficult to isolate which were the most critical in bringing about any change. For example, you may have been enthusiastic about the new teaching method and this enthusiasm communicated itself to the learners. But next week you might not be so enthusiastic. The class troublemaker might have been off sick and there were no disruptions to deal with. Or maybe what you were teaching was of special interest to the learners, etc.'

Sam's reflection

15 September

I think my research focus is OK. But I probably need to refine it a bit more. I'm still not sure if I want to collect data from the learners on what teaching methods they like or if I'll just collect data from teachers. I can't start writing my research questions until I'm absolutely clear about what it is I want to explore. That's like setting off on a journey before you decide on a destination.

I'm glad that my research questions can be open-ended. I like the idea of exploring, investigating or analysing an area of work rather than having to provide a single answer to a specific question.

This education research isn't what I expected. It seems much less abstract than the sort of research you see reported in TV programmes like 'Horizon'. But then, that's scientific research and education research deals with people and what they say and do. It's bound to be different.

I've just realised it's because I'm dealing with people that I can never prove cause and effect. You can never know why people act in a particular way. What they do may be the same but the reason they do it can differ. So a teacher might shout at a misbehaving learner because they have a headache, they had a row with their partner or the head has just told them off. It may have nothing to do with the learner's behaviour.

Review of tutorial

Writing my focal paragraphs and research questions

'Now,' said Richard 'research questions are difficult to write and there are a number of things that you need to think about. Wilson (2009a) has some good advice on this. Personally I always suggest that you start by writing a **focal paragraph**. That's a short piece, no more than a page long – shorter if possible – which outlines the area that you want to research, where you are going to do the research, why you want to do the research, how you are going to do it and why it's worth doing. You can use it like a compass to keep you on track as the research progresses. From this focal paragraph you draw out your research questions. Regardless of the length of the project or dissertation I think three or at most four research questions are enough.'

'But, if I'm writing 15,000 words, won't I need more questions than if I am writing 5000 words?'

'You'd think so, but the truth is that within any research question there will be a number of issues. The more words you have to play with the deeper you can delve into each of these issues. Even a PhD at 80,000 words will probably only have four or five main research questions, but each will be explored in great depth.'

'So what you're saying is that as you progress further in your studies you go deeper into each question and the issues within it rather than increase the number of questions.'

'Precisely. And as you'll see "going deeper" is one of the things that separates Level 6 from Master's level work.'

'So what makes a good research question?' I asked.

'They have to be clear and explicit to both you and your supervisor. Both of you need to know what it is that you're trying to find out. They also have to be doable. For example, what's wrong with the following question: "I wish to identify the factors that limit the potential of five students identified as gifted and talented"?'

I wasn't at all sure that I had an answer but suggested, 'It's a bit vague'.

'It's more than a bit vague,' Richard replied. 'How do you define and measure potential and what is meant by gifted and talented? Are they gifted, talented or both? What limitations are you talking about? Are they physical, mental, sociological or all three? It is a really complex question that would be a nightmare to research. No, what you have to do is keep it simple, focused and manageable in the timescale available. Remember KIS – keep it simple.'

'I thought that was KISS – Keep it simple stupid!'

'It was until one student complained,' Richard replied, his eyes looking heavenwards.

Sam's reflection

16 September

Clearly writing my research questions is not something that I can just dash-off in a spare ten minutes. I need to think some more about which aspects of teaching methods I'm most interested in. Then I need to write my focal paragraph and think carefully about the precise research questions that I want to investigate. I also need to keep the number of research questions I set myself to a manageable number. Three seems to be the magic number.

Review of tutorial

How am I going to collect my data and how much do I need?

'So you have an idea about what you want to investigate. The next question is who are you going to collect data from?'

'I could start by reading the OfSTED report and then collect information from the teachers and the head. And if I wanted to know which teaching methods the learners liked most or least, I could ask them.'

'Leaving the learners aside, how do you intend to collect the data?'

'There are about 60 teachers, so I can't interview them all. I would use a **questionnaire (➡ Tutorial 7)** and then **interview (➡ Tutorial 6)**, say, six teachers.'

'How long will each interview last?'

I hadn't really thought about that so I suggested, "Half an hour".

A slight smile touched Richard's lips and he tugged his ear. 'Each half-hour interview will generate about five pages of single-spaced A4. That's at least thirty pages of transcripts or about 13,000 words of text. Not to mention all the data from your questionnaires.'

My mouth didn't drop open but it felt as if it had. That much! Never!

'How long is your assignment?' he asked.

'Five thousand words,' I replied.

'I suggest you issue a questionnaire to all the teachers but support this with say three short **semi-structured interviews** with teachers, or maybe a **focus group (➡ Tutorial 6)**. I'd also suggest that you dump the idea of collecting data from the learners, otherwise you will be drowning in data.'

Access and insider research

'How about carrying out research where I work, is that OK?'

'Yes of course it is. Why do you ask?'

'No reason really, I just thought that I might have to carry out the research outside of my normal workplace for it to be acceptable.'

'No there is no such requirement. What you are doing is called "**insider research**". Hockey (1993) wrote a really good article about the joys and problems of insider research. You should look at it before we talk about **ethics**. Personally, I'd argue that one of the major strengths of your project is that you have easy access to the people you want to research. That makes life much easier. I once had an MA student who wanted to research the leadership style of a friend who worked in the Royal Navy. His friend was happy to be observed in action, but it took six months for the student to get the security clearance required to board one of Her Majesty's nuclear submarines. Needless to say his assignment was late! So always check that you have access before embarking on the project. You will need to confirm with your line manager that you have permission to undertake the research and **informed consent (➡ Tutorial 4)** from all those who take part in the research.'

'What's informed consent?'

'Good question. As I said earlier we'll talk about ethics later but for now you need to remember that you can't demand that anyone take part in your research. If you ask your class or colleagues to fill in a questionnaire, you have to make it clear that they have the right to refuse and if they do take part they have the right to withdraw from the research at any stage.'

'OK,' I said.

Why my research is worth doing and more on data collection

'Now, we're really starting to get to grips with the issues,' Richard said, leaning forward. 'We have an idea about the what, the where and the how. The next thing to think about is why are you doing this research?'

I felt like saying, 'because it's part of the course,' but instead said, 'Because it's a problem at work'.

'Good. Solving a practical problem or doing a piece of research that will improve your professional practice is always a sound reason for a teacher to undertake a piece of research. But when will you collect your data?'

'I'll have to do it when things are a bit less manic. I was thinking of just before Easter.'

'Remember the hand-in date for this assignment is the 30th of June and you'll need time to write up your findings. Therefore I suggest that you collect the data a little sooner, maybe mid-term. You will need the help of your colleagues to distribute, administer and collect in the questionnaires, so time your data gathering to minimise any disruption that your research might cause them. That way you won't annoy them and they may even agree to take part in any future research you undertake. Once you have a date, you can work backwards and draw up a research plan and timetable. And don't forget to think about how you are going to disseminate your findings.'

Disseminating my findings

'I hadn't planned on presenting my findings. I was just going to give the head a copy of my report.'

'I'd encourage you to share your findings with colleagues, perhaps at a staff training day. It's really important that teachers disseminate their research to colleagues: that way good practice and increased understanding of the issues can be shared. Think about doing a presentation at one of the school's training days. Anyway, I seem to have been doing a lot of talking. Do you have any questions for me?'

'Do I have to include copies of the completed questionnaires and interview transcripts as an appendix in the final work?'

'Increasingly, because of plagiarism, universities do ask that you include copies of completed questionnaires, interview transcripts and observation schedules. So do it.'

Sam's reflection

16 September

It is obvious that I've seriously underestimated the amount of data that I'd collect from six interviews, not to mention the questionnaires. I need to think about the ways that I might reduce the size of my research. I will definitely drop the idea of collecting data from the kids. After that my options are:

➡

- sending the teachers a questionnaire rather than interviewing them;
- restricting the research to just teachers in years 9 and 10;
- collecting data from just a sample of teachers, e.g. from only assistant heads and above.

I really need to think some more about what my primary research interest is.

I was glad to hear that I can carry out the research in my own workplace. I remember a previous lecturer banging on about the need to always carry out research outside our normal environment. His argument was that it helped you to be objective. Clearly Richard disagrees. Maybe I'll ask him about this when I see him next.

But I'm not keen on presenting my findings to other teachers. I mean I'm new to teaching – what do I know?

Review of tutorial

Working at Master's level

'Anything else?'

'If I decide to study this module at Master's level what do I have to do differently from what you have already said?'

'Sorry I forgot about the levels. Did you have a look at the handout I gave you?' (see pages 20–1).

'Yes, but I'm not sure I understood the jargon.'

'It is pretty heavy going, I must admit. But basically what you have to do is make certain that you achieve all the Level 6 descriptors. Now you have a first degree, so you must have already demonstrated an ability to critically review a coherent body of knowledge, and evaluate a range of theories, data, and concepts. At

Level 7 you have to go deeper in terms of critically reviewing the ideas of other and evaluating both **primary data** and **secondary data**.'

'What's primary and secondary data?'

'The terms can have different meanings depending on how you use them. In this instance primary data is stuff you've collected say from your questionnaires. Secondary data is material you have read. But primary data can also be the raw data such as statistics you collect, while secondary data is what those statistics become when you have manipulated them in some way.'

'OK,' I said.

'In addition to the Level 6 criteria you have to display intellectual skills at Master's level in terms of a complex body of knowledge and/or skills. Demonstrating a superficial knowledge of a topic is not sufficient. You have to demonstrate a real depth of knowledge and understanding. After all you are supposed to be a *master of your subject*. For example, if you were a GP you would have some knowledge about a very wide range of illnesses. But the consultant your GP sends you to will have a very deep knowledge about a small specialised area of knowledge such as the liver.'

'So it's about depth not width of knowledge.'

'Exactly. As for the process element of the descriptors you can clearly see that research lies at the heart of Master's level studies. That's not to say that you can't study a taught module at Master's level and write an essay on it. What it implies is that primary and/or secondary research plays a significant part in most Master's level programs.'

'Like when you do your dissertation?'

'Yes. But also in taught modules where you will undertake secondary research to find the books and articles you need. Lastly, in terms of accountability you are expected to become a more **autonomous learner** at Master's level than at undergraduate level. It is essential that you assume a greater responsibility for your own learning and the decisions you make. You have to do the work. No one will be standing over you making you do the work or spoonfeeding you with ideas and suggestions. Your supervisor will offer advice and support but only you can decide whether to accept it or not. You should also be able to demonstrate a growing willingness and ability to guide and lead other professional staff and initiate action rather than wait for instructions. Which is why dissemination of your findings is even more important at Master's level than at Level 6.'

'That's a bit clearer. But specifically in terms of what we discussed tonight what do I need to do differently if I go for Level 7?'

'In this instance not a lot. The early stages of research are the same whether you are studying for a degree, masters or doctorate. You have to identify your focus. This you can only do after you have done a bit of reading around the topic. Then you can identify what you want to do and where are you going to do it. After that you need to identify your research questions and, based upon those, how you intend to collect your data. Of course, if you are studying at Master's level, everything you do will have to be more robust.'

'Robust?'

'Yes. You need to ask yourself is the focus of the research suitable for study at Master's level? When I say that, I don't mean that it has to deal with a more complex and difficult issue than a Level 6 project. Rather your subject must have sufficient depth for it to generate enough quality data for you to **analyse** and **critically evaluate (➡ *Tutorial* 3)** both your primary and secondary data in some depth.'

'So we are back to depth not width.'

'Correct. At both levels you have to report your findings. But at Master's level your write-up must contain a higher percentage of analysis and critical evaluation than at Level 6. If the data you collect is lacking in quantity, quality or depth you won't have the raw data you require to work with.'

'So, it's a case of picking a nice juicy topic to get your teeth into?'

'Exactly. You want a full, four-course spread and not a quick snack! In addition, you will have to spend more time at Master's level justifying the choice of your topic. At undergraduate level it might be sufficient to say that the research is of interest to you and that it will improve your professional practice. At Master's level the work should be of interest to a wider professional audience in the form of a presentation, lecture or article.'

'You mean it has to be publishable?' I said, with something like fear in my voice.

'No. I'm saying the topic and the findings should have the potential to be turned into a publishable article or a conference paper.'

'Anything else?'

'You will need to spend more time considering your research methodologies, strategies and methods because . . .'

'It's them that provide the data you are going to evaluate and analyse,' I said.

'Yes. But, you will also have to fully justify why you choose the methodological approach you did. Therefore, you have to understand the other options that were available to you and have a good reason for rejecting them.'

'OK. I see what you mean by "more robust". My thinking and shaping of the project has to be more thorough and comprehensive.'

'Exactly.'

'What about originality. Does work at Master's level have to be original?'

'Definitely not. You can do a project on a subject that has been looked at a thousand times. Master's level study in education isn't about discovering new knowledge, it's about exploring a professionally relevant subject in order to understand what is going on and possibly making a contribution to improving professional practice.'

'Which is another reason why I need to disseminate my findings.'

'Yes.'

Sam's reflection

16 September

I'm beginning to understand what the difference is between Level 6 and Master's level but it's not entirely clear yet. Obviously I need to decide at what level I'll undertake my research. But I don't have to make my mind up now.

I suppose, if you got a First for your undergraduate degree, then your powers of analysis, critical review and evaluation of theories, ideas and other data must already be very good. Whereas if you have a 2:1 like me, you'll need to do a bit more work getting up to Master's level. But from what Richard said it's not a huge step-up.

We spent the final few minutes discussing what actions I needed to take before the next meeting, and before we finished Richard gave me a ➡

copy of his Tutorial Record, which summarised the main points covered in the tutorial. It was a diagram headed 'Starting to research' and a copy of his handout 'Research Checklist Schedule' which he said I should use to help clarify further my thinking and the focus of my research. The Schedule looks useful if a bit long-winded. But he did say that it was something I should work on over a period of time and update as my thinking evolves.

Overall, the session went as well as I could have expected. After the first few minutes I was able to relax and listen to what Richard had to say, and using the recorder was a really good idea. I've learnt so much from just listening to the tape again. And I've been able to write in sub-headings on the transcript to help me find stuff I need. But I don't like the sound of my voice.

One thing that has surprised me was how supportive Richard was. I don't know why he would be different to the other lecturers. Maybe it's just his title, Research Supervisor. It sounds so formal. Anyway, now that I have broken the ice I might be relaxed enough next time to ask a few questions.

Record of tutorial

Student: Sam Sylon   **Date: 15/9/XX**

SUMMARY OF KEY LEARNING POINTS

What is research about?

Research is not just about proving something or discovering new knowledge. It can be about exploring common everyday situations. It's a way of learning that involves the collection of data from other people, and one of its purposes is to improve the researcher's professional knowledge and/or practice.

KIS – Keep it simple. Don't be overambitious

A good piece of research needs to be self-contained and doable in the time available. Make sure that you have access to a site where you can collect your data. Doing your research where you work makes it easier for you to obtain permission to do the work and collect the data. But avoid collecting too much data; much of it you will never be able to use because of the word limit.

Focal paragraph/s

Summarise in about 200 words the subject of your research, where and how you will carry out the research and why it's worth doing.

Research questions

Once you have a clear statement that describes your research, identify three aspects of the issue that you particularly wish to explore. These will become your research questions. A good research question will be:

- clear, concise and focused;
- a sentence or so long;
- of personal and professional interest;
- manageable in the time available.

One research question might be enough for a short project, two or three for a 5,000-word assignment and maybe three or four for a long project or dissertation over 10,000 words.

Working at Master's level

You have to go through the process described above regardless of the level you are working at. However, research at Master's level is more concerned with depth of knowledge than breadth. Therefore the topic chosen must have greater potential for in-depth study than that which would be acceptable at Level 6. The research approach adopted needs to be more robust in terms of identifying your research aims, focus and approach. The quantity and quality of the data collected must be sufficient to enable you to interrogate it in sufficient depth to meet the criteria required for Master's level study.

➡

A very good assignment at Master's level should have the potential to be publishable once it has been amended to meet the requirements of a journal article. Those articles that don't meet the standard required by **peer-reviewed journals** may find a home in a **professional journal**.

Work at Master's level does not have to be original or discover new knowledge. However, if you carry out research in your own organisation, the results will be unique to that organisation at the time you undertook the research.

Agreed action points

Sam will:

- Complete the 'What' and 'Why' sections of the Research checklist schedule (Handout 1.2);
- Visit the library and look at how journal articles and dissertations are structured and written.

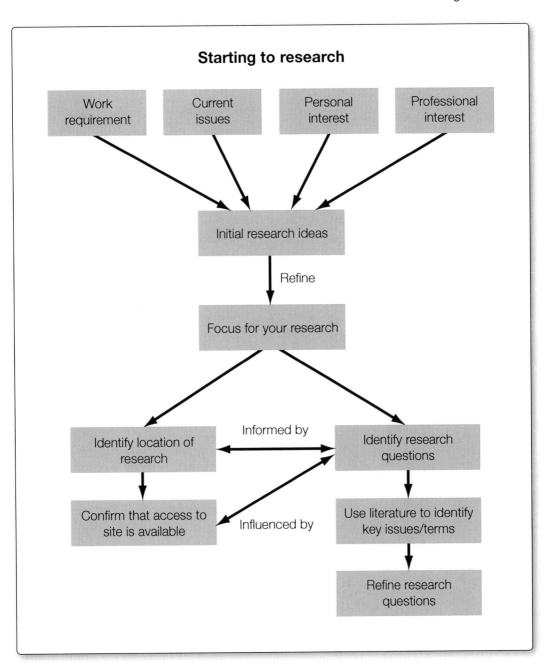

Handout 1.1

ACADEMIC QUALITIES

The following table describes the academic qualities that students are
expected to demonstrate at Level 6 and Level 7 and is based upon the National
Qualifications Framework for England and Wales. If working at Master's level
you must demonstrate both the skills listed under Level 6 and 7.

National Qualifications Framework – Level 6 and 7 descriptors

Descriptor	Level 6	Level 7
Intellectual skills and attributes	Critically review, consolidate and extend a systematic and coherent body of knowledge. Utilise highly specialised technical or scholastic skills across an area of study. Utilise research skills. Critically evaluate new information, concepts and evidence from a range of sources.	Display mastery of a complex and specialised area of knowledge and skills. The key word here is 'mastery'. You have to convince the reader that you fully understand your area of study. Demonstrate expertise in highly specialised and advanced technical, professional and/or research skills. The key word here is 'expertise'. It's not enough to use the skills. You must demonstrate a high level of skill in their use.

Descriptor	Level 6	Level 7
Process	Transfer and apply diagnostic and creative skills in a range of situations. Exercise appropriate judgement in a number of complex planning, design, technical and/or management functions related to products, services, operations or processes including resourcing.	Conduct research, or advanced technical or professional activity using and modifying advanced skills and tools. You must be able to adapt the tools at your disposal to the unique demands of your work. Design and apply appropriate research methodologies. It is essential that you fully justify your choice of research methodology and demonstrate why it was the best approach to adopt for your research. Communicate results of research to peers. Dissemination of findings to peers is something all Master's students should aim to do. Develop new skills to a high level, including novel and emerging techniques. Act in a wide variety of unpredictable and advanced professional contexts.
Accountability	Accept accountability for determining and achieving personal and/or group outcomes. Begin to lead multiple, complex and heterogeneous groups.	Accept that you are accountable for the decisions made in the research process including how you have used feedback given to you by supervisors. Take significant responsibility for the work of other professional staff; lead and initiate activity.

Handout 1.2

RESEARCH CHECKLIST SCHEDULE

Use the following questions to help you think about your research. Start each question on a new sheet of paper and provide as much detail as you can. You should amend and update the schedule as your ideas evolve and if required it can be used as the basis for your research proposal.

What?

Summarise in plain English the aims and objectives of your research. Write a short statement that describes the focus of your research. List your research questions.

Why?

Why do you want to carry out this research? What is its purpose? Why is it worth doing? (Remember that research into a topic of professional interest will very often improve your professional knowledge and practice).

How?

How do you intend to carry out the research? Will you use interviews, observations or questionnaires?

Where?

Where will the research take place? Do you have access to this location? If you have to negotiate access, how long will it take?

When?

When will you conduct the research? How will you monitor your progress? Draft out a realistic timetable that allows for delays and use it to monitor your progress. The first entry on your timetable should be the deadline for completion/handing in. Work back from that date.

Ethics?

Have you obtained and read the British Educational Research Association (BERA) ethical guidelines free from **www.bera.ac.uk**. You will need to discuss the ethical issues raised by your research with your supervisor.

Impact?

What will be the impact of this research, on your pupils/students, school/college/university and/or your professional practice?

HOW TO STRUCTURE YOUR RESEARCH REPORT

Aim of tutorial

To provide you with guidance on how to structure a research report and the content of each section. Some readers may find aspects of this tutorial challenging because it introduces jargon which is commonly used in the research process. All of this jargon is defined in the glossary. If you find the tutorial heavy going we suggest you skim-read it. This will provide you with an idea of what you are aiming to write. You can return to the tutorial later when you are more familiar with some of the terminology used.

Areas covered in this tutorial

Sam's reflection

28 September

I was looking forward to my meeting with Richard. I'd done my homework and I had a number of queries that I wanted to raise with him.

Review of tutorial

Academic writing style

When I entered, Richard was talking to a colleague on the phone about Albion's win at the weekend. He seemed in a good mood. He waved me into a chair and I sat down. These sessions were proving to be much more informal than I had expected.

'Sorry about that Sam,' he said, hanging up. 'How have you been?'

'Confused,' I said. 'I did what you asked and visited the library to look at how research reports and dissertations are structured but they seem to differ from report to report. Some of them are even written in the first person.'

'What's wrong with writing in the first person?'

'It doesn't sound very academic.'

'So you think a research report needs to be written in a formal academic style to be acceptable?'

'Well, yes.'

'Don't confuse good academic writing with formality, complexity and the use of long words. Sometimes it seems to me that some academics write in order to show how clever they are. Thankfully others write in order to communicate their ideas. I prefer the latter. Therefore, my advice is to avoid trying to write in an academic manner and instead write as clearly and unambiguously as you can. To help you write clearly I suggest that you never use a long word where a shorter one will do. In addition keep sentences under 20 words. Any sentence longer than 20 words is probably two sentences and, unless you are a grammarian, the longer a sentence is the more chance there is that you will get the grammar wrong. The current record for a sentence that I've marked is 168 words! That's a paragraph. It's commonly accepted amongst journalists that there are far fewer grammatical errors in tabloid newspapers, which use short sharp sentences, than in broadsheets which use many more compound sentences. So remember – apply the KIS principle and Keep It Simple.

'Similarly with paragraphs,' he continued. 'Each paragraph should only deal with one issue or point. This means that some paragraphs can be very short while others are much longer. As for writing in the first person, it's perfectly alright to write in the first person. It sounds far more natural to say "I found that . . ." rather than to say "The researcher found that" . . . but we can talk about this more when we discuss **quantitative** and **qualitative** approaches to research.' (➡ *Tutorial 4*)

'That sounds good to me,' I said.

Sam's reflection

28 September

What is this man on that he keeps a record of the longest sentence he has ever marked? Get a life! Mind you, I found what he had to say reassuring. I've found some of the writing, especially in the academic journals, heavy going. I suppose reading articles is a bit like going to the gym. At first it's really hard but as your fitness improves it becomes easier. I have to get my mind fit. Mind you, it was nice to hear that I didn't have to write like that. What I need to do is write clearly and unambiguously and I can even write in the first person if I want to. Great.

Structure of a dissertation or research report: the title

'So what's the proper way to structure a research report?' I asked.

'OK,' he said. 'Have a look at McMillan and Weyers (2010) and McGrath and Coles (2011); they've both got some interesting things to say about writing your project or dissertation. Just remember that there are different ways that you can structure a report, and you should always check out the house style of the university you're at, including how they feel about you writing in the first person. But, broadly speaking, there are certain key features that appear in all reports, regardless of what they might be called. So, let's start at the beginning. How important do you think the title is?'

That seemed an obvious question. 'Very important,' I replied.

'Why?'

'Because it needs to tell the reader what the research is about.'

'That's one view. But what if I told you that it wasn't very important?'

'I'd disagree with you.'

The front pages and abstract

'OK, let's leave that for the moment. What follows the title?'

'A table of contents and a list of all the tables and figures that you've used. Oh, and a list of any appendices.'

'Correct. And what follows that?'

'The introduction.'

'Before that?'

'Oh, you mean an **abstract**.'

'Exactly. Abstracts are hard to write and I suggest that you leave yours until you have finished writing up your research. The abstract needs to summarise in about 200 words what the research is about and what the key issues and findings are. It is not something that you can dash off in ten minutes. A good abstract can take several days to write.'

'But I can't afford to spend days writing 200 words,' I said, louder than I'd intended.

'I didn't say that you had to work on it eight hours a day. What I meant was that you need to write and rewrite your abstract over a period of about an hour. Then put it in a drawer and forget about it for a few days, then take it out. Read it again and make any changes that you think are required. Then repeat the process until your abstract presents an accurate summation of your research.'

'So, what you're saying is that I need to reflect on what I've written and change it as required.'

'Correct.'

The introduction – and my focal paragraph

'Then it's the introduction,' said Richard. 'So what are you going to write about in the introduction?'

'Well, I suppose I explain what the research is about.'

'Precisely. You write your focal paragraph. We touched on that last time. (➡ *Tutorial 1*) Have you written your focal paragraph and revised your research questions?'

I gave him what I had completed and he spent a couple of minutes reading it and writing comments in the margin.

'This is pretty good,' he said. 'Your focus is sharper than it was and you've clearly decided that what you're interested in is finding out what teaching methods the teacher uses and which they think are the most effective. The advantage of providing a sharper focus for your research is that you won't collect inessential data, which means you can spend more time analysing the data you do collect. You can also dig deeper into it because you have less data to analyse. Your focal paragraph makes it clear to the reader what the work is going to be about. Well done.'

'What about my research questions?'

'They're a lot better. You've got rid of the question marks and they are clear and unambiguous.'

Sam's reflection

28 September

I felt relieved when he said the focal paragraph and research questions were OK. I'd put a lot of effort into them. I certainly think that the changes I made capture more clearly what I want to do and most importantly I think it's going to be easier. Because now I'm exploring what people do and think rather than discovering the single best approach to teaching a bunch of learners.

Review of tutorial

Titles (again)

'So now you have an abstract, a focal paragraph and your research questions. What do they do?'

'Oh, I know where this is going. You're going to tell me that because I have outlined what my research is about in both the abstract and the introduction my title doesn't have to do that job.'

'Correct. People spend too much time worrying about titles. Keep it short and relevant but don't try and summarise your entire research project in the title. I once had an MA student whose dissertation title was half a page long.' He grimaced at the memory.

The introduction continued – where will my research take place, with whom and how will I collect my data?

'So what's next?' I asked.

'You need to tell the reader where the research is going to take place and who your participants are going to be. So, briefly describe the setting in which the research will take place. Is it an inner city school or in the leafy suburbs, how many staff and learners does it have, what percentage of the learners receive free school meals or speak English as a second language. That sort of thing. But there is one thing you should never do. Any ideas what it is?'

I sat and thought for what seemed like an age, then I realised what he was on about. 'All of the articles I read gave some background about where the research took place but none of them named the organisation in which it took place.'

'Exactly. They didn't use the organisation's real name or the names of any of the participants. They protected their respondents' **anonymity. (➡ Tutorial 4)** You must do the same. Then you can tell the reader who it is you are going to collect data from and how you intend to collect it. For example, you might say "In order to collect my data I intend to issue a questionnaire to all teachers in the school and hold a 25-minute, semi-structured interview with three senior teachers", or whatever.'

Why my research is worth doing

'Now, having outlined what your research aims are, where the work is going to be undertaken and how you intend to do it, it's time for you to say why it's worth doing. Usually it will be because it's of professional interest and will help you to improve your professional practice. However, it might just be a subject that has always fascinated you. So you need to write another paragraph or two explaining your motivation.'

'What if I'm only doing it to pass the exam?'

'Then I suggest you're economical with the truth,' he said, smiling.

'You mean lie?'

'You might say that, I couldn't possibly comment.'

Outline the remaining content of my report

I grinned and moved on. 'What else goes in the introduction?'

'You need to do what all good teachers do. In every lesson you tell your students what you are going to cover in the session, you cover it and then you tell them what you've covered. It's the same with your report. Very briefly, you outline the remaining contents of the report. For example: "in the Literature Review I explore the literature that relates to teaching methods in secondary schools. The **research methodology (➡ Tutorial 4)** section outlines the reasons why I have adopted a qualitative approach and used questionnaires (➡ *Tutorial 7*) as my primary data collection tool. The findings contains a summary and analysis of the data I have collected and the conclusion summarises my three most significant findings, discusses weaknesses in my research and identifies areas for further study."'

'Hang on, are you saying I should point out the weaknesses of my research in the conclusions?' I asked, surprised. 'Won't that reduce my mark?'

'No, it's good practice. No piece of research is perfect. What you need to demonstrate is that you are aware of how your work could be improved. That sort of critical self-reflection will gain points not lose them and it's especially important at Master's level.'

Sam's reflection

29 September

Thinking about it, I realise that most of the examples I've looked at followed the format suggested by Richard. They had an abstract and the introduction set out what the report was about and what the purpose of the research was. However, not all of them explained the layout of the rest of the work. I think they should have. After all, it does help the reader to know what's coming next and to skip it if they want to. But I'm not so sure about revealing the weaknesses in my research. I'll have to think about that a bit more.

Review of tutorial

The literature review

'OK,' I said, 'so then it's the literature review?'

'That's right. Now we'll have a full tutorial devoted to the literature review (➡ *Tutorial 3*), so for now we will just do a quick overview. What goes into a literature review?'

'Anything that you've read that is relevant to your study,' I said, confidently.

'No. That is not a good idea. As you progress up the academic ladder, you'll learn more and more about whatever it is that you're studying. Very soon the word limit for the assignment will stop you from reporting everything you know about the topic. That's why you have to be selective and only include material which is relevant and up to date.'

'So I need to exercise some judgement and select material that has a close correlation with my research questions?'

'Correct. As you climb up the greasy pole of academic studies you'll find that what you leave out becomes just as important as what you put in. You have to exercise judgement and discretion in terms of what to exclude...'

'And let me guess – this is even more important at Master's level.'

Critical evaluation, analysis and synthesis of literature used

'Yep. In addition, where there's more than one side to an argument you need to report the differing views. I can't emphasise enough how important it is to **evaluate** the literature that you use and not just accept what one writer says.' (➡ *Tutorial 3*)

'Won't giving all sides of the argument use up a lot of words?'

'Not if you're selective and avoid using long quotes. Try to summarise the arguments in your own words and do remember to reference the source of the ideas. Use short powerful quotes to emphasise a particular point that you want to make. If you're really good you can take the arguments of two or more writers and **synthesise** what they say on a particular subject.'

'What do you mean by "synthesise"? Is it similar to analyse?'

'When you were a child did you ever play with Lego bricks?'

I nodded yes, mystified where this was going.

'Me too, and when you became bored with the house you built you took it apart?'

'Yes.'

'Well that's analysis. You select an argument, some data or a theory, and you take it apart brick by brick. Synthesis occurs when you take the same bricks and build something new. What was a house now becomes a stable or an airplane.

You can do the same with theories. You can pick two or more theories, take them apart and then reassemble them into a new or revised theory.'

'That can't be easy.'

'No, it isn't, but if you can do it you will score well in any piece of academic writing.'

Selecting the literature to use

'So, in the literature review I need to select the most appropriate literature that deals with my research topic. But how do I check that it's appropriate?'

'Easy. except for **seminal** or really important books and articles only use literature that has been published in the last five or six years.'

'If I do that, won't I miss out lots of important writers?'

'I'm not saying you can't use older references, but use them sparingly. Very often later writers summarise what previous writers have had to say on a subject and that can be useful. However, world-renowned writers have got there because of the power of their message and it can be really revealing to read their original work, no matter how old it is.'

'OK.'

'Secondly, either use the literature or lose it! What I mean by that is – the literature review is there to help you understand and analyse your findings. So, if you don't use a reference in your findings you need to ask yourself: why have I included this in the literature review? The theories and ideas contained in the literature review are there to help you explain, explore, confound or support your findings. That's one of the purposes of the literature review. However, there is one type of literature that you may need but which you may not refer to in your findings. What do you think it is?'

I must have looked blank because after a short pause Richard said 'Background information. That's information which contextualises the issues. For example, you might want to briefly outline government policy on an issue before you get to grips with it in your institution.'

Sam's reflection

29 September

What Richard said about the literature review seems to make sense. But I still suspect that I'll collect far more literature than I can use. If I'm not careful the literature review will be huge. It looks like I'm going to have to learn to edit my work. But what if I cut something out by mistake? I'd better think about how I'm going to save different drafts on the computer.

Nor do I feel comfortable criticising the work of published authors. After all they're the experts. How am I supposed to criticise them? Maybe the easiest way for me to do this is to compare and contrast what different writers have to say on the same subject.

Review of tutorial

The research methodology

Outline of the research methodology, strategy and data collection methods that I've used

'After the literature review comes the research methodology section, which is crucial to any piece of research. In it you have to demonstrate that you're a competent researcher and that you understand a range of research methodologies (➡ *Tutorial 4*), strategies (➡ *Tutorial 5*) and data collection tools (➡ *Tutorials 6 and 7*) and issues associated with carrying out research.'

'So it's a practical section where I describe what I've done?'

'Partially. You'll need to outline what you've done but you'll also have to justify your choice of methodology and methods and to do that you need to understand some research theory. Again, we'll look at this in detail in future sessions, but basically I suggest that you start the section with a summary statement such as: "the research methodology that I adopted was *qualitative* in nature, the research strategy was that of a *case study*, the methods used to collect data included *observation*, *questionnaires* and *semi-structured interviews*".'

I must have appeared confused because, without waiting for me to say anything, Richard continued speaking. 'What you need to do is define each of the words or phrases that I've emphasised (in italics) and discuss their strengths and weaknesses. So, in this instance you would have to talk about qualitative research, case studies, observations, questionnaires and interviews and explain why you've used each of them.'

'But what if I don't want to do qualitative research, whatever that is?'

'I'm sorry, I haven't made myself clear. I'm not suggesting for a moment that you have to use these precise methodologies, strategies and data collection methods. It's just a format that you can use to start the methodology chapter. Like a maths formula, you can drop anything you like into the phrase. Don't worry about the terms at the moment; you don't have to decide on what approach you're going to take until later.'

Sam's reflection

30 September

I remember thinking at the time that it was alright for him to say 'don't worry', but my head was ready to explode. I was hanging on by my fingertips. But I consoled myself with the thought that it would all become clear when I've had a chance to review my notes and listen to the tape. So far my theory is not working! In future if I don't understand something I must ask him to go over it again.

Review of tutorial

Dealing with the issues of bias, ethics, generalisability, reliability, validity and triangulation

'Then you need to write a paragraph or so on each of the following concepts: **bias**, **ethics**, **generalisability**, **reliability**, **validity** and **triangulation** (➡ *Glossary and Tutorial 4*). Again, we'll discuss what each of these terms means later, but you may want to look them up before then. If you do, use the index and not the table of contents to track down the various entries under each heading. That way you will spend less time ploughing through the book and also learn how these terms can change as the circumstances in which they are applied change.'

Use a range of textbooks and summarise what you did

Grasping at straws and trying to slow down the delivery of information, I asked, 'I know that you gave me a list of four highly recommended texts, but how do I choose which one to use as my main back-up to *Your Education Research Project Companion*?'

'What suits one person very often doesn't suit another. The best thing to do is to visit the library, or a good academic bookshop and have a look at them. There is nothing like handling the text, flicking through the pages and reading extracts for finding one that suits you. It is also essential that you use at least two different texts because . . .'

'You should never rely on one person's viewpoint,' I said.

'Exactly.'

'OK, I'll visit the library and check them out. I need to have a look at what journals they have anyway.'

'Good idea. Once you have dealt with the theory surrounding your research approach, you need to briefly outline what you did and the order in which you did it. This can be done in the form of a table if you are short of space. Make sure that the theory matches the practice. For example, if you said that you used interviews under data collection methods, make sure that you talk about interviews and not observations when outlining what you did!'

'Surely no one makes that mistake?'

'I've seen it happen several times. People write their research methodology before they undertake their research. Then, during the research they change their minds about the focus of their project or the tools they will use to collect data. But they don't go back and rewrite the methodology section to reflect these changes.'

Sam's reflection

30 September

As I'm writing up these notes I'm starting to realise that what Richard was giving me was a framework for how to lay out a research methodology chapter. The details about what goes into each part will come later. For now I don't have to worry about what the terms mean. It's enough to know that there's a template that I can use. In many ways the summary statement at the start of the research methodology chapter is like my introduction at the start of the lesson. It summarises what will be discussed in the chapter. But it also acts as a kind of checklist reminding me of the issues that I must cover.

Review of tutorial

The findings and how long each section should be

'Then it's the findings.'

At last, I thought, 'something that isn't technical.'

'The findings and conclusion sections are the crux of any research assignment. They represent the creative element of your work and, as such, they should account for a minimum of 50 per cent of the work.'

'So how's the other 50 per cent divided up?'

'Good question. I'd use about 5 per cent for the abstract and introduction, 25 per cent in the literature review and 20 per cent for the research methodology, 40 per cent for the findings and 10 per cent for the conclusions. These are a guideline and your research may differ. But if you find that only 20 per cent of your assignment is given over to the findings and conclusions, there's probably something wrong with it.'

Sam's reflection

30 September

At the time I didn't think much about what Richard had said but, on reflection, it's actually very useful. Not only does it provide guidance on how much goes in each section, it also enables me to break the task down into small chunks. Whichever Level I opt for my 5000-word assignment becomes six mini tasks, the longest of which (the findings) is about 2000 words. That makes life easier. I can manage that.

Review of tutorial

Writing up my findings

'Is there any particular way that I should write up or organise my findings?'

'A lot depends on what your findings are. When you've collected some data we can discuss how best to report the findings (➡ *Tutorials 8 and 9*), but essentially what you need to do is to introduce the chapter by briefly explaining the scope and content of the section.'

'Oh, we're back to telling them what you are going to teach them, tell them and tell them what you've taught them,' I said, feeling pleased with my understanding.

'Exactly. You then need to take each of your findings and analyse them. Remember to use your literature review to do this. So, for example, "As Parker

(20XX) predicted I found that . . ." or, conversely, "In contrast to Parker (20XX) I found no evidence for his claim that . . ."'

'So what you're saying is that I have a conversation with the literature.'

'Precisely. You use it to explain, explore, support and challenge your findings.'

'But what about my own analysis? Doesn't that count for anything?'

'Indeed it does. However, you must support your interpretation by reference to the literature or the data you've collected. You can argue a case for a particular interpretation of the data but it must be both reasonable and logical. Otherwise it is just your opinion. And that's not worth much in an academic paper, although it might make you a living as a journalist, where the facts are seldom allowed to get in the way of a good story – or the story the reporter wants to sell.'

'That sounds cynical.'

'Maybe. But remember,' he said, smiling, 'a cynic is just a disappointed romantic. Besides, academic writing is about arguing a case and supporting it with evidence not opinion. It is good practice to follow Hayek's advice and present the strongest argument you can against your own views and then demonstrate why your arguments are superior.'

'That sounds like a lot of work.'

'It is, but it's also what distinguishes good academic work from the average. We'll talk about findings some more when we consider analysis of data.'

Referencing material

It sounded as if Richard felt strongly about this issue so I changed the subject, asking 'Is there anything else I need to do in the findings?'

'Yes, and this applies to your literature review as well. Reference all material correctly. If you don't already have the guide to referencing from the library, pick up a copy while you are over there. We use the Harvard System here but you may be used to a different system. Every college or university will have a particular model and it's important to know which system is used and to follow it.'

'But why's it so important?'

'There are a number of reasons. Firstly it helps you to avoid **plagiarism**. If you don't acknowledge where you got an idea or a quote from you could be accused of passing off someone else's work as your own. That is probably the greatest sin that an academic can commit. With the new plagiarism software that universities now have it's easy to spot. Secondly, when marking your work I might want to follow up an idea that you are writing about. Without a reference I wouldn't know where to start.'

'But why would you want to follow up an idea of mine?'

'It may be new to me or perhaps I think that you have misquoted or misunderstood what the writer said and I want to check up on it. Thirdly, good referencing is a sort of quality guarantee. If you reference material carefully, the chances are that you will also have been careful with other aspects of the work, while poor referencing might indicate that you've been equally slapdash in the conduct of your research.'

'So I need to get it right?'

'Absolutely. You'll seldom fail an assignment because of poor referencing alone but you will lose marks.'

Writing my conclusions

'So now we're onto the conclusions.'

'Yes. It's essential that your conclusions flow naturally from your findings, so make sure that there's coherence between what you say in the findings and what you discuss in the conclusion. You would be surprised how often the two don't match up. In the conclusion you talk about what you have learnt as a result of carrying out the research. It won't be possible to cover everything so pick out your three most important findings and identify areas for future research.'

'What about recommendations? Are they the same as conclusions?'

'No. Conclusions are discursive. Having carried out your research you discuss what you have learnt. Recommendations are far more directive. With a recommendation, you indicate what action you want the reader to take. For example, you might write: "It is recommended that teachers adopt more learner-centred methods of teaching such as . . ." It's quite common for research projects to only have conclusions, but occasionally people may want to make recommendations. But don't do as one misguided undergraduate did and include a series of recommendations addressed to the government!'

'Anything else?'

'No new literature or findings should be introduced at this stage. You should only comment on what you've written about in the previous pages. And remember to discuss any weaknesses in your research.'

'Oh we're back to highlighting my mistakes?' I said, knowing that it would get a reaction from him.

'No it is not like that. It is about you critically evaluating the quality of research. That is an essential skill for any researcher. No piece of research is perfect. There will always be ways in which it could be improved. Besides, anyone marking a piece of research will want to see that you're able to critique your own work. Far from losing you marks it is likely to improve your score. Remember that this sort of course is intended to train you in basic research skills as well as how to design and carry out a piece of research.'

Sam's reflection

30 September

There's a lot to take on board from this session. But now that I've had the time to go over the transcript twice I can see that there is a lot of useful information in it. There are obviously different ways of writing up research but it's essential to include all the main elements (abstract, introduction, literature review, research methodology, findings, which includes analysis, and conclusions). What Richard has provided me with is a template that I can fit my data into and embellish it with subheadings as required.

Working at Master's level

'We're nearly out of time so let's look at working at Master's level,' Richard said. 'Did you have a chance to read last week's handout about working at Master's level?'

'Yes, but I'm still not entirely sure of the differences.'

'OK. Have a look at this (see Handout 2.2). It describes what you have to demonstrate in an assignment to pass at Master's level. I think it's easier to understand than just looking at the descriptors and, of course, the better you can do what's suggested the higher your mark will be.'

'I'll have a look at it,' I said. 'But in terms of what we've just discussed what do I have to do to raise my work to Master's level?'

'The major problem I have with new Master's students is that they try too hard. They wrongly assume that the step-up from undergraduate degree to Master's is huge so they try to be "academic". They use a big word when a small one will do. They write in jargon and supply several references for each point they make when one or two would be sufficient. They construct elaborate theories to explain data when an obvious interpretation of events is staring them in the face...'

'Why do they do this?' I asked.

'Lack of confidence, I think. They want to show how hard they have worked. So they try to cram everything they know about the subject into their assignment, with the result that it's long on description of theories and data but short on critical evaluation and analysis. As we have just discussed, they fail to appreciate that at Master's level what you leave out of an assignment is as important as what you include. Such judgement takes time to develop.'

'If I do the study at Master's level what criteria should I use to decide what to include?'

'You need to have a very clear research focus and set of research questions. Then you can evaluate every piece of data or literature on the basis of "does this item help me answer my research questions?" If it does it can be included. But if it's merely interesting rather than essential, you either have to discard it or include it as an appendix. You also have to ensure that you make frequent and meaningful links between theory and practice.'

'You mean link the theories in the literature review with my findings.'

'Exactly. Einstein once said that great art was the expression of complex ideas in a simple form. That's what studying at Master's level is all about. Reporting, explaining and analysing complex ideas in a simple format that an intelligent lay-person can understand. It's not about making things complex. The best Master students see the Master's as an extension of their undergraduate studies, not as a mountain to climb. They read widely and exercise judgement about what to include in their assignments.'

'But isn't it a waste of time to read widely if you know that you can't include a lot of what you read in your assignment?'

'That's a fair question. But I can always tell if a student has read widely or just worked through the 10 or 20 references they use in the text. When you read widely, the knowledge goes into your subconscious and composts down. Even if you don't reference it in your assignment, it informs your thinking and improves your analysis, evaluation and interpretation of the literature and data. It helps to make you a Master of your subject and not someone who just wants the letters MA after their name. Also, being practical, at Master's level you have to do more reading around the subject before you can define your research focus.'

'Because you need to be certain that the topic has sufficient depth to support a study at Master's level.'

'Yes.'

'Does the format of the research report stay the same?' I asked.

'What I've outlined is fairly standard but there are variations on it, so always check out just what your supervisor wants.'

'Such as?'

'Well, some supervisors and universities like you to write separate findings and analysis sections. Personally I think this is a waste of words because in the analysis you have to refer to the findings again before you can undertake any analysis.'

Sam's reflection

30 September

I'm going to have a good read of the handout Richard gave me. It does seem easier to understand than the document he gave me last week. I particularly like the fact that it's split into two sections. The first part lists what I have to demonstrate in order to be awarded a pass at Master's level and the second part lists what I should be able to do.

The rest of what Richard had to say was basic common sense. The last time I was at home Dad was on about how the Japanese manufacturers don't try to make huge improvements to an entire production process. Instead they just try to improve each part of the process by 1 per cent. This results in a massive improvement in overall terms. That's what I have to do. Improve each part of my work by a little and remember to KISS (Keep it keep simple stupid).

Record of tutorial

Student: Samantha Sylon   **Date: 28/9/XX**

SUMMARY OF KEY LEARNING POINTS

The following elements are required in a research report.

Title page

Table of contents

List of figures and tables

List of appendices

Abstract (approximately 200 words)

Introduction (approximately 5 per cent of word count)

- Define the question or scope of the topic that you are writing about (focal paragraph).
- List your research questions.
- Describe the setting in which the research will take place.
- Identify your research participants and how you will collect data from them.
- Explain why you are interested in this particular topic and justify why it is worth investigating.
- Outline the remaining content of the assignment. ➡

Review of literature (approximately 25 per cent of word count)

- Introduce the section by briefly explaining the scope and content.
- Remember that this is a critical review of the literature and not just a report of what you have read. Compare and contrast the different views of the writers you use.
- Reference material correctly – see Student's Handbook and/or the Information Services guide to writing references.
- Avoid using excessively long quotes. Only quote if the form of words is critical to the message. A summary of the writer's opinions in your own words is more valuable than a long quote – anyone can copy from a book.
- Avoid plagiarism at all costs.
- Check that the material is relevant. If it's not used to explain/explore your findings, why include it?

Research methodology (approximately 20 per cent of word count)

The research methodology section is a crucial element of your assignment and one that people can struggle with. This summary suggests one way that this section can be structured, but it is not the only way!

- Start with a summary of the research approach that has been adopted, e.g. 'The research methodology was *qualitative* in nature, the research strategy was that of a *case study*, the methods used to collect data included *observation*, *questionnaires* and *semi-structured interviews*'.
- Define what is meant by each of the words italicised above and discuss the strengths and weaknesses associated with that approach, strategy or method.
- Explain how you have addressed the following:
  - Bias
  - Triangulation
  - Validity and reliability
  - The analysis of data
  - Ethics.

- Describe what you actually did. Remember that this is a vital part of the methodology. Someone should be able to repeat your research from the information that you provide.

- Provide a timeline, in the form of a table, to guide the reader through your research process.

- Provide a short conclusion that considers the strengths and weaknesses of the approach taken in the light of experience and what might be done differently if the research were repeated.

Findings (approximately 40 per cent of the word count)

- Introduce the section by briefly explaining its scope and content.

- Discuss one point at a time and link the various issues to be discussed with linking phrases such as 'In the above section I considered the motivational impact of transformational leadership. In this section I shall explore how transformational leadership can be employed to exploit staff.' Use linking words and phrases such as 'conversely' and 'in contrast with'.

- Link findings back to issues discussed in the literature review, e.g. 'As Grayson (20XX) predicted I found that . . .'

- Reference all material correctly.

Conclusions (Approximately 5–10 per cent of the word count)

- It is essential that conclusions flow naturally from the findings.

- No new literature or findings should be introduced at this stage.

- Use the Rule of Three to:

  - Outline the three most important findings from the research.

  - Comment on any areas of weakness in the assignment.

  - Identify areas for future research.

List of references

Appendices

Agreed action points

Sam will:

- Speak to the librarian and identify the full range of resources, paper-based and electronic, that are available to students and how to find them.
- Check out what journals are available in the library and online.
- Obtain and read a copy of the library guide to referencing.

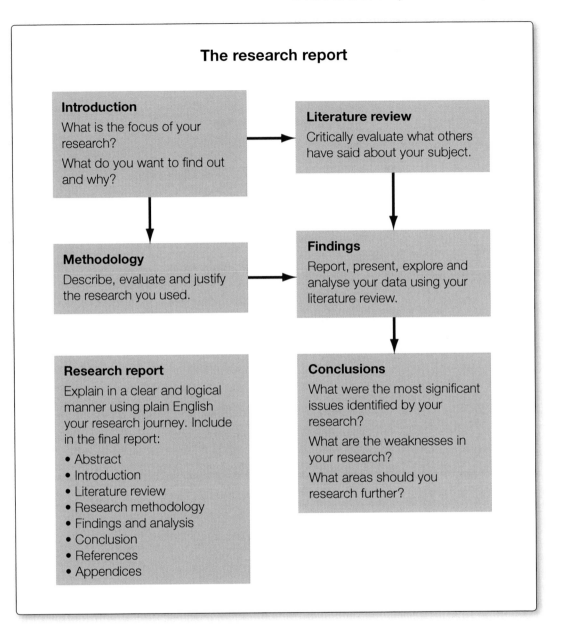

The research report

Introduction

What is the focus of your research?

What do you want to find out and why?

Literature review

Critically evaluate what others have said about your subject.

Methodology

Describe, evaluate and justify the research you used.

Findings

Report, present, explore and analyse your data using your literature review.

Research report

Explain in a clear and logical manner using plain English your research journey. Include in the final report:

- Abstract
- Introduction
- Literature review
- Research methodology
- Findings and analysis
- Conclusion
- References
- Appendices

Conclusions

What were the most significant issues identified by your research?

What are the weaknesses in your research?

What areas should you research further?

Handout 2.1

PRESENTATION OF RESEARCH REPORT

What follows is some general advice on how to ensure that your assignment is well presented, clear and logical.

- Check what the course requirements are as regards font size and spacing. This is normally size 12 double spaced. Use size 16 bold for main headings and 14 bold for subheadings.
- Use subheadings within chapters to organise your material.
- Use bullet points in moderation.
- Carry out a spell and grammar check of your work prior to final submission. A red wavy line means that a correction is required (don't ignore it as many students do), and a green line indicates that you need to review the grammar.
- Ensure that your work is logically structured and not haphazard. If you find that your work jumps from issue to issue and back again, it is likely that your structure is weak. Planning is vital here. Consider using flow charts or mind maps to improve the organisation of your work.
- Never use a word or phrase the meaning of which you are unsure. If in doubt use a dictionary.
- Never discuss a theory that you don't fully understand.
- Check that you have no sentence longer than 20 words. If you do you probably have two or more sentences.
- Only one issue should be discussed in a single paragraph. Remember: one point = one paragraph.
- Keep it simple. Good academic work is all about discussing complex ideas in a simple and clear manner.

Handout 2.2

DESCRIPTORS FOR QUALIFICATION AT MASTER'S LEVEL

Degrees at Master's level are awarded to students who demonstrate the following:

- A systematic understanding of knowledge and a critical awareness of current problems and learning in their academic discipline.

- A comprehensive understanding of techniques applicable to their own research or advanced scholarship.

- Originality in their application of knowledge (note this does not imply new knowledge: for example, applying a theory in your unique setting or applying a nursing theory in an education setting would meet this requirement).

- An understanding of how established techniques of research and enquiry are used to create and interpret knowledge in their discipline.

- An ability to evaluate critically current research and advanced scholarship in their discipline.

- An ability to evaluate and critique a range of research methodologies and, where appropriate, propose new hypotheses.

Typically a holder of a Master qualification will be able to:

- Deal with complex issues, make judgements in the absence of complete data and communicate clearly their findings to specialist and non-specialist audiences.

- Demonstrate self-direction and originality in tackling and solving problems and act autonomously in planning and implementing tasks at a professional level.

- Demonstrate an ability to advance their own knowledge and understanding and develop new skills to a high level.

- Exercise initiative and personal responsibility.

- Demonstrate decision making skills in complex situations.

- Demonstrate a commitment to continuous professional development.

Adapted from The Framework for Higher Education Qualifications in England, Wales and Northern Ireland.

WRITING YOUR LITERATURE REVIEW

Aim of tutorial

To introduce you to the notion of a conceptual framework. Specifically it provides guidance on how to find and evaluate relevant literature, structure and write up your literature review.

Areas covered in this tutorial

Sam's reflection

11 October

From what I've heard the literature review sounds difficult. In the last tutorial we started to discuss how to find literature on theories relevant to my project. So I need to be clear about the focus of my research and the theories that relate to it.

My project is about teaching methods, so I need to define what I mean by teaching methods and identify a range of methods that teachers can use. Richard mentioned the idea of finding a single book or article that I could hang my research on. Fortunately I found McGrath and Coles (2011) on my first visit to the library just by wandering around and looking at what was on the shelves. How lucky was that?

Review of tutorial

Richard was all business when I entered. As soon as he had finished saying hello he said 'Right, so it's the literature review now?' He probably had an appointment after me.

'Hmm. This is going to be the worst part of my project,' I said.

Finding a key text

'No, it's fascinating. It's when you start to uncover the different perspectives of a topic. There are some good books to help you. Have a look at Hart's (2001) on how to do a literature search and his earlier book from 1998 on how to do a literature review. They are both very comprehensive so don't get bogged down in them – read selectively. You should also look at Wilson (2009b). Anyway, I suggested that you have a browse in the library. Did you find anything useful on teaching methods?'

'I had a look at your recommended reading list and I noticed that the book by McGrath and Coles (2011) is for PGCE students. It covers writing assignments and teaching in Secondary and Post Compulsory Education and it had a good section on teaching methods. Is that OK?'

'That's not a problem. In fact using theories from different education sectors can often throw light on our professional practice. Besides, there is a lot of overlap between teaching in further education and secondary schools. But as we've said before you can't rely on just one or two books. The main thing is that you have found a recent book that opens the door to literature relevant to your topic. Now you can start to search for other publications in a similar area. Hopefully the book will have given you some new key words to use in your searches and an idea of the key concepts that you need to look out for.'

Two ways to structure a literature review

'The McGrath and Coles certainly helped me identify key words. They mentioned teacher-led and student-led teaching methods and give extensive examples of both. Could I structure my research around these two themes?'

'Indeed you could. The two most common ways to structure a literature review is chronologically, meaning you discuss the literature in the order in which it was published, or thematically. I often suggest that students should use their research questions as subheadings in both the literature review and the findings. That way the topic is automatically broken down into manageable sections. This also makes it easier to have that all-important dialogue between the literature and the findings when you're trying to analyse (➡ *Tutorial 10*).'

'I like the sound of that. My findings could be organised thematically as a mirror image of my literature review.'

Sources of literature to search

'Indeed they could. But let's not jump the gun. You're developing your **conceptual framework** and have some useful key words. What you need to do now is to start your literature search. Remember that you need to aim for diverse sources. Very often key words vary between writers. You say that McGrath and Coles uses the terms "teacher-led" and "student-led" teaching methods, but other writers may use the term "teaching styles". So you may need to play around with different combinations of words.'

'OK,' I nodded.

'Now government reports are often really useful as they can change policy or influence how teachers operate. So, it's also a good idea to look at selected websites such as the Department for Education (DFE), Ofsted or the National Foundation for Educational Research (NfER), as they will almost certainly have published reports on relevant topics. Then there are periodicals such as professional magazines, *The Times Educational Supplement*, union publications and those from subject associations. These are all sources of useful information. Once you've looked at these, you can begin your electronic search for reviews and journal articles.'

'But won't I have enough already?' I said as a vision of drowning in paper crowded into my mind.

'Hopefully the documents that we've discussed will be critical, but they don't always compare and contrast different views. For that you need a wider range of writers. Remember that critical appraisal is a very important aspect of working at Level 6 or 7 (➡ *Tutorials 1 and 2*). The point about academic journals is that they'll help you to develop your critical skills. They often promote a particular viewpoint, but it should be supported by appropriate evidence. Your task will be to consider whether you think that the evidence provided supports the writer's viewpoint or not.'

'I'm not sure that I can do that. I mean, how do I know who to believe?'

'It's not so much "who to believe", but whether you think that the evidence supports the judgements made by the writer. There are a few tricks here to help you. You can consider the provenance of the authors and the source.'

The provenance of literature

'What do you mean by provenance?'

'Provenance means the origins, but in this case it's a bit more than that. If you take information from a website, how do you know whether the person producing the webpage has sufficient knowledge and experience to present a valid viewpoint?'

'I don't. But academic papers are reviewed by other academics, so I should be able to trust them more than websites, shouldn't I?'

'Probably. But it's a judgement you have to make. However, there is a hierarchy of journals. Some publishers have better reputations than others. At this stage you can't be expected to know which are the strongest, but this expertise will develop in time. Certainly most journals in college and university libraries are a reasonable bet because someone has had to justify their purchase. Here, you can have this handout in which I have ranked the sources of literature in order of how reliable they are' (see page 73.)

'There's a lot here. Do I have to use one example from each source?'

'No, not at all. It's just a list of the sources that you might use.'

'What about the provenance of websites?'

'You have to exercise judgement when using a website. Always look at who is hosting the site and when it was last updated. Try and determine if it is advocating a particular political position or theory and take this into account when deciding if it's worth using.'

'OK.'

'Even with literature from reputable sources you always have to decide how much you can rely on what they are claiming. You might want to look at the methodology described in the paper and decide whether you think it was valid and reliable (➡ *Tutorial 4*).'

Undertaking a literature search

'How are you going to start your literature search?' Richard asked.

'I thought that I'd Google my key words and identify some more sources.'

'Well, that's not a bad idea. However, I would recommend that you use Google Scholar because it focuses on academic and peer-reviewed sources and includes abstracts. The great thing is that the articles are ranked by the number of citations each has attracted, so you tend to get the most popular ones first. You can even click on "Cited by" and see all the documents citing a particular source.'

'Right. So if I were to enter Wilson or Hart as a search term I would see all the people who had referenced their work, and of course those books and articles would be more up to date than their original work.'

'Exactly. It's also worth mentioning the Web of Science and the Arts and Humanities Citation index. These are electronic citation indexes usually available in most university libraries. You can enter a publication and they give you a list of publications citing your original source. There are also specialist search engines such as the British Education Index and the British Humanities Index. Some websites provide subject specialist links too, like "Socioweb" and "Intut". I also like "Zetoc", which lists the contents pages of most journals. It's an easy way to keep up to date on what's being published. It's always worth checking the electronic resources available in the library. Just go and have a play. You will be amazed at what you find.'

'OK. But what about just going to the library and physically looking at the books and education journals?'

'Actually that's a very good idea. Once you know the subject area that you're interested in it only takes a couple of hours to have a quick look at all the relevant books and journals in the library and identify which ones cover your specific interests. Once you've identified which are useful you can go through the contents page of each and identify any relevant material.'

'How far back should I go?'

'If you go back five years you will very quickly identify any seminal books or journal articles that were published earlier, because everyone will be referencing them. You can then decide if you need to read the original works.'

'A colleague told me that what he did was find one really good article and then he used the list of references at the back to trace other relevant books and articles and then used their lists of references to expand his search.'

'You can do that, but writers very often reference other writers who agree with their own views and arguments. What does that do for your literature review?'

'Makes it unbalanced?' I said doubtfully.

'Correct. It could infect your work with bias as you would be relying too much on one article and the references the writer used to support their position.'

'I was right. The literature search isn't straightforward.'

'Don't worry about it. There is no perfect way to do a literature search. Most students use a mixture of wandering around the library with purpose and using the various electronic search engines that are available. And the most important word in that sentence is "purpose". It really is a question of deciding what you need, then choosing the most appropriate method of searching.'

'But I'm still worried that I could miss a vital article.'

'Actually that's unlikely. If you read four or five up-to-date relevant articles they will probably list 80 plus references between them. Any seminal work in your area is very likely to be in that list. It's like Gary Player, the golfer, used to say, "the harder I work, the luckier I get". It's the same with you. The more you search the better your literature review will be.'

Sam's reflection

11 October

Who the hell is Gary Player?

Help! I'm going to drown in literature. There's an awful lot of stuff out there that I need to be aware of and I can't read it all or use it all in my project. Stay calm. At least now I've an idea where to look. With so much to plough through I can see why it's important to clarify my terms and concepts at the start. The correct key words and combination of words will limit the amount of material that I have to look at.

Review of tutorial

Keeping track of what I've read

'I'll have to find somewhere to keep all this paperwork so that I can find what I need when it comes to summarising the information and writing my literature review,' I said. 'Have you got any hints I could use?'

'Well, there are a few tricks that might help. You should write the literature review as you do your research. Don't wait until the end to start writing. That way, what you write will feed into the planning of your research and the analysis of results. So do it a bit at a time. I know that the literature review seems like a daunting task, but you don't need to summarise the whole article or book. You just need to summarise what's relevant to your studies.'

'But how do I know what's relevant?' I asked, despairingly.

'You need to keep referring back to the focus of your research, your research questions (➡ *Tutorial 1*) and key words. It helps to break it down by starting with subheadings relating to your individual themes. For example, you might have headings for teacher-led methods of teaching, student-centred methods of learning and Bloom's Taxonomy. You can then file your notes under these categories. It really helps if you keep a record of each reference and a brief summary of what it contains. You can use a database such as Access or specialist software such as EndNote – we'll talk about these later – or a separate Word document for each category. You could even use old-fashioned index cards. McMillan and Weyers (2010) have some good advice on keeping track of what you've read.'

Save time – read selectively

'This all sounds good in theory but I'm still not convinced. Potentially I have a mountain of literature to read and I don't really know where to start.'

'Selective reading is the key. It's a good idea to consider what you want to get out of a source before you read it and make a list of points. You'll find that similar points relate to several sources, so you won't have to develop a different list for each piece of literature – you'll be able to adapt your basic list. Then read the part of the document that is relevant to what you need to know.'

'How do I find the bits I need to read?'

'Think of the sections that you find in a research paper. How could you use these to identify what you should read?'

'I suppose the abstract would tell me whether the source is worth reading at all; maybe the introduction would do that too. The literature review would cover the concepts if that was what I was after. It seems like cheating, but I could read the conclusions and skip the rest!'

'Indeed you could. You could also use the subheadings and skip those that seem irrelevant. The problem is that you can't always be sure what is irrelevant, so try skimming through some sections and reading others more carefully. Check to see if the report has an executive summary. If so, read that first.'

'You sound just like the trainer I had on my speed reading course. She said that we have to read strategically and that we need to develop a range of reading strategies, including skimming, reading just the introduction and conclusion and just checking for key words and phrases. Then, if I decide it's important, I can read the document more carefully.'

'She was right. But once you do identify important information, remember to highlight it. You can do this with a highlighter pen on hard copies but you can also do it electronically onscreen. But remember to use different colours; that way you can colour-code different themes.'

'I hadn't thought of that,' I said.

'You can even copy selected quotes directly into your literature review file, but be very careful and use a different font colour so that you don't include someone else's work as your own accidentally. Remember . . .'

'Avoid plagiarism at all costs,' I said.

Using quotes and summarising what I've read

Richard smiled and nodded. 'That's another reason why it is vital to record each reference accurately, particularly the page number in the case of direct quotes. Remember to only quote when the form of words is such that the meaning would be changed if you were to summarise it; otherwise paraphrase.'

'Can you give me an example of what you mean?'

He was silent for moment, thinking, and then lent forward. 'OK,' he said, 'Jimi Hendrix is alleged to have said "Knowledge speaks, but wisdom listens". It's a great quote. It's short, sharp and powerful. It would be impossible to paraphrase it without losing impact. So you would use the quote as it is. However, faced with a page of government prose you could probably summarise it in your own words and lose none of the meaning. Just remember that, if you use a long quote, all you've done is prove that you can copy. If you summarise the information in your own words accurately, you're demonstrating that you understand what's been said. But sometimes you need a quote because it captures in a forceful way exactly what you want to say. Which brings us back to Jimi. Are you a fan?'

Sam's reflection

11 October

I thought it was best not to tell him that Jimi was my father's generation and side-stepped his enquiry. I wonder if he plays air guitar to 'All along the watchtower'? Now there's an image that I don't need in my head.

I've been worried that I'd have to read loads of material and then sift through it all again when it came to writing my literature review. But Richard's suggestion that I summarise as I go should eliminate the need to read everything twice. But I must remember to note down the full reference of any book or article that I intend to use.

Hang on, I've just had a ping moment with light bulbs flashing! If I have my sources gathered in files – paper and/or electronic – under themes relating to my research and I have highlighted all the important points (I must be selective here and not highlight everything or I'll never see the wood for the trees), I can start to write about each theme by just reading the appropriately colour-coded text.

I should start by trying to organise my literature sources into a logical order. I can always move text around, so it's not vital that I get the order correct at the very beginning especially as I may need to include new themes as a result of my reading, or even delete some. Anyway, I can always use my old friend 'cut and paste' to help me. Later I can add quotes, but only if I feel that they're really relevant and add impact to what I'm saying.

Review of tutorial

Critical evaluation of literature used

'Of course, all you've done so far is describe what's in the literature; you must also evaluate it critically.'

'I guessed that was coming. Just as I thought that I'd cracked it, there's more to do. I hope that you've got an answer to that one too!'

'I don't pretend to have all the answers, Sam. I'm really just describing an approach that works for some people. You'll need to adapt it to your style of working. A critical approach is best taken when you've had a chance to reflect on your writing for a week or so.'

'So I should allow some time between reading something and critically evaluating it?'

'Yes. After your little break I suggest that you re-read what you've written and make a note of the various views about each issue. Reference each view with the author's name. Then look at your notes and organise similar views together. You can now go back to your quite descriptive account and add phrases like: "x agrees with y on this issue because . . ." but "in contrast, z took a different view namely . . ." This approach might seem long-winded, but you'll soon get used to it and you'll get better at it with practice. But don't expect writers to hold diametrically opposite views. Very often in education the differences between authors is fairly slim, but they are important and you need to identify them.'

'Basically I have to compare and contrast what different writers say?'

'Exactly. But you should also consider how appropriate their data collection approach was, especially if you are working at Master's level. You must ask yourself does the data they collected support their claims and is their interpretation of the data reasonable. An awful lot of ideas in education are based on little or no empirical data whatsoever. Instead they are someone's bright idea or their own professional practice. If you don't believe me look at the Coffield Report on Learning Styles (2004) and you will see that most learning style theories are not based on any empirical research at all.'

Sam's reflection

11 October

I had a ping moment at work today – I must be on a roll. I can record my literature review on an A3-size mind map. I could do it on the computer but I like to see the whole picture in one go. That way I can ➡

keep track of what I do, and see the links between different parts of the literature review. Maybe this would be useful for other sections too, such as the findings.

Being critical is obviously important. Given the number of words I have for the literature review it seems obvious to me that my main approach will be to compare and contrast what different authors said about a subject. But I should also try and challenge some of the literature on other grounds as well, such as lack of supporting research or the author making illogical deductions based on the data collected.

I'm surprised that most education theories are not based on actual research. It really means that much of what we are taught about teaching is open to challenge. I think I'll have a read of Coffield's Report. I'm sure it will be on the Web somewhere.

Right, I'm off to bed. I can listen to the next section of the tape tomorrow.

15 October

So much for listening to the tape the next day. Claire was off sick and I had to cover her classes for three days. Talk about panic. What with trying to plan her lessons and get the resources organised I barely had time to turn around. At busy times like this I must try and do a bit of study each day, even if it's only 15 minutes. That way I can keep the momentum going. I know from experience that if I leave a piece of work too long I find it hard to get back into it. Still, back to normal now.

Review of tutorial

Referencing

'Now we need to talk a bit more about referencing. Can you remember why referencing is important?' (➡ *Tutorial 2*)

'You gave me three reasons last time. Firstly, it helps you to avoid charges of plagiarism. Secondly, the reader can follow up any of your references if they're interested or think that you've misrepresented the text. Thirdly, you said that it gave the reader confidence in what you'd written. Because, if your referencing was done correctly, it would be likely that you'd also been careful with how you evaluated the literature and wrote up your findings,' I said, feeling pleased that I'd checked my notes the previous night.

'Very good! You're right about plagiarism. It's easy to accidentally include material from another author, so it's important to re-read your work. Markers are very experienced at recognising a change of "voice" in a piece of work and they will often Google a sentence to see if it has been copied. It's also increasingly possible that your work will be checked against anti-plagiarism software. So, guard against innocent plagiarism. We find that some overseas students think that they are honouring an author if they just copy the writer's work. But that doesn't show any criticality at all, it's just copying. OK, it sounds as if we can leave referencing . . .'

'Hang on. I have a few questions.' Richard nodded for me to continue. 'I'm not at all sure how often I need to reference. For example, if I use the same source several times in a paragraph, do I need to reference it every time?'

'There's no fixed rule here. If it's clear from your writing that you're still discussing a particular source, then you don't need to reference it again. If desperate, you can use **ibid.** – literally this means "the same place" – which means that the points under discussion come from the previously cited source. But don't use this too often as it can become tiresome to read.'

'Suppose the author I'm reading refers to someone else's work and ideas. If I want to refer to those how do I reference that material?'

'It's good practice to only cite sources that you have actually read in the original. When we find students referencing a source that they haven't read in the original, we say that they have cited "indirectly". It's not a great problem if it only happens on the odd occasion, but if you do it repeatedly it becomes an issue of academic integrity because you're implying that you've read something when you haven't. What you have to do is use the phrase "cited in" as part of the reference: for example, Banner cited in Benjamin and Grimm (20XX). The reference relates to Benjamin and Grimm's work. But if you do this too often it gives the impression that you're lazy and couldn't be bothered to read the original source.'

'OK, I accept that referencing is important but I found it really annoying recently when a tutor made a load of comments about my use of first names and book titles in the text.'

'Following the conventions of referencing is important because people have an expectation that something will be done in a particular way and, if it's not, confusion can result. For example, it is really difficult for someone else to follow up your work if the references are incorrect. And it can affect the readability of your work if your argument is interrupted by too much detail like first names or titles of articles.'

'So it's really all about good academic manners?'

'Correct! When it comes to the style of referencing, most universities have their own preferred approach and you must stick to it. This university uses the Harvard System, which is author and date in the text and the author/s family name and initials, date of publication, title, and details of publishers and place of publication in a list at the end. This list is always in alphabetical order by author's name. If there's more than one publication by an author, they go in chronological order. If there are two or more publications by the same author in the same year then you use "a", "b", et cetera to differentiate the texts. In the text you can quote up to two authors for a single source, e.g. Banner and Bruce (20XX), but if there are more than two authors, then you name the first one followed by "et al.", which means "and others", but you list all the names in your list of references. Most people aren't too fussy about details such as whether you use commas after names or pg or p for "page", but the important thing is to be consistent. Anyway, all the details are in the library guide to referencing. Have you picked up a copy yet?'

'I've picked up a copy already.'

'Good. Next you need to read it!'

'I have,' I said, defensively. 'It said that bibliographies and footnotes shouldn't be used. Why's that?'

'Again these conventions differ from one university to another, so it's always worth checking. A bibliography is a list of sources that you've consulted, but not taken specific information from. Some universities, like ours, prefer that you only list those sources that you have cited in your work. Footnotes aren't used in the Harvard System and, besides, they interrupt the narrative flow, and if a point is worth making it is worth making in the main body of the report.'

'Are there any computer packages that will help me do my references?'

'There are several. For example, EndNote. This is an example of a biblio-graphic package. It's designed to help you store, summarise and integrate your references in your writing. But you could just keep an electronic list or even a database using Access or Excel. However, EndNote is designed for the purpose and you can present your references in any chosen format. You can get stu-dent versions, but it takes time to master. So, if you're only managing a small number of references, a manual system on Word, Excel or index cards will be sufficient. However, if you have 50-plus references and you are intending to con-tinue researching, it may be worth learning how to use a package.'

'OK. What about indenting quotes?'

'Again, convention varies and the rules aren't too strict on this, but short quotes of under 30 words can be included in the text in quotation marks with a citation and page number. Sometimes italics are used to distinguish such quotes from the student's work. Longer quotes are usually given a separate paragraph and indented. But what have I said about long quotes?'

'You told me not to use quotes unless the form of words is critical, so I suppose that long quotes aren't popular.'

'Not popular at all! Sometimes we get work that consists of a string of quotes. You can imagine that this doesn't score too highly. Or a quote suspended between two paragraphs with no indication of which paragraph it refers to. A col-league of mine calls these "hanging quotes" and he hates them.'

'I suppose any assignment that's just a string of quotes lacks criticality.'

The difference between tables and figures

'Absolutely! Now while we're talking about the layout of your work, what's the dif-ference between a table and a figure? (➡ *Tutorials 8 and 9*)

'A table is a table and a figure is a **figure**,' I responded, sounding like a charac-ter out of *Alice in Wonderland*.

'A table is a table, but what's a figure?'

'Now you've got me!'

'Anything that's not a table.' Now Richard sounded like a character out of *Alice*.

'You mean **graphs,** diagrams, pictures and **charts**?' I asked.

'Exactly! Again, this may sound pernickety, but it's important that your work communicates your meaning effectively. Remember that half the battle of academic writing is getting your message across – communicating and explaining complex ideas clearly and concisely – and there are conventions for this. So a table is a table and it is labelled in the text as "Table 1" et cetera. You may also see "Table 2.1". This convention is used in longer accounts and it means that the table in question is Table 1 in Chapter 2. This helps the reader to find the table without looking through the whole account. This convention is applied to figures, too. Don't forget to add a legend to tables and figures.'

'You mean a title?'

'No, a title usually goes at the top of a figure and is very brief. A legend goes underneath and it provides a little more information than the title.'

'But it's unlikely that I'm going to use either tables or figures in my literature review,' I said.

'Maybe. But if you are talking about an issue the meaning of which is contested or has multiple definitions, such as the aims of education or education leadership, you can easily summarise what a range of writers have to say on the subject in a table and save words.'

Writing a literature review at Master's level

'OK. So what's different about writing literature reviews at Master's level?'

'You have to do everything we have discussed above but you have to do it at a higher level. This is where some of Hart's (1998) ideas can be really helpful. Basically, you need to be more critical, more sceptical about the claims that writers make for their work. Jeremy Paxman of *Newsnight* fame was once asked what is he thinking about when he's listening to a politician answer one of his questions. His response was that he always thinks "Why is this ******* lying to me!?" You have to do the same. You need to ask: why has the writer said this? Is it because he wishes to promote his own agenda, build an academic reputation or simply sell some books?'

'So really it's a matter of questioning everything I read.'

'Yes. In addition, if we go back to the handout I gave you about what students have to demonstrate at Master's level (➡ *Tutorial 2*) you have to show that you have a "systematic understanding of knowledge and a critical awareness of current problems, (issues) and insights" of the subject you are studying.'

'What do you mean by "systematic understanding"?'

'Teachers and lecturers collect a lot of information about their subject and teaching and learning from talking to colleagues, reading various materials and even finding stuff left on the photocopier! But that knowledge was not collected in a structured fashion. It's a haphazard approach. Therefore, you may not fully understand an issue, because you are missing some essential information. Systematic understanding comes from studying a subject in a planned fashion.'

'So you get the full picture and not just half of it.'

'Correct. In addition, you have to demonstrate that you are at the forefront of your academic discipline. So you need to be up to date. What does that mean for your literature review?'

'I need to use up-to-date literature.'

'And where do you get the most up-to-date literature from other than a good website?'

'Journal articles.'

'Correct. So any assignment at Master's level needs to be rich in journal articles. Even at Level 6 you need to include some journal articles but at Master's level they are vital. Journal articles usually contain the most up-to-date ideas on what you are writing about, and to demonstrate mastery of your subject you have to be familiar with the latest ideas. Anyway, that's enough for today.'

Sam's reflection

16 October

Much as I find referencing a pain in the neck, it's pretty clear that it's important. Especially with all the attention that universities are giving to plagiarism. I suppose I'll have to try once and for all to crack the problem. I imagine that once you have learnt how to reference properly it becomes second nature and you don't even have to think about it. Anyway, I hereby resolve to read and learn the Harvard System. Then I ➡

can become one of those people who are always harping on about poor referencing and how it is indicative of a drop in academic standards.

I'm beginning to understand what studying at Master's level entails. It's really about cultivating a questioning state of mind. It's far too easy to go through life not questioning what we see on TV and read in the newspapers. You only have to go abroad to see how the same events are reported very differently in, say, France compared to England. So why do we believe that what's written in books and journals is the only interpretation of the issues discussed.

If I do the Master's I have to make certain that my literature search is well structured, up to date and accurately captures the current views on teaching methods. No problems there then! I'll also have to get really stuck into the journals.

Record of tutorial

Student: Sam Sylon   **Date: 11/10/XX**

SUMMARY OF KEY LEARNING POINTS

It is essential that you:

- Identify a clear conceptual framework as early as possible as this will help you focus your reading.
- Find a seminal source that 'opens the door' to the literature.
- Identify key words and phrases that you can use in your searches.
- Start your literature search with a visit to the library. Spend some time just reviewing what journals and books are available in your area of interest. Explore what electronic resources and searches are available and remember to act with 'purpose'.
- Start writing your literature review immediately. As your research progresses this will inform and be informed by your findings.

- Identify the key themes in your work and organise a filing system for recording relevant material. As an aid to identification use colour coding.

- Be critical. Don't just accept what the writer says; ask yourself why s/he has said it. Is it based on evidence or is it just their bias or ideology talking?

- Follow referencing conventions.

- Avoid plagiarism at all costs.

- Use quotes sparingly.

- Consider using a bibliographic package. For small-scale research projects they are unnecessary. A manual system or a simple database will do. However, knowing how to use them is a useful transferable skill.

- Number and label figures and tables correctly.

- Check the university guides for guidelines on presentation of work.

- Have a look at **http://scholar.google.co.uk/**.

- If you decide to work at Master's level, ensure that your literature search is systematic and that you identify and use the seminal books and articles in your area of study. Remember: if in doubt ask your supervisor. That's what I'm there for.

- At Master's level your literature review needs to contain more journal articles than books. Articles are more up to date than books and will focus on a specific issue, unlike many books which cover a wider remit.

- Critical evaluation is vital at Master's level. Simply describing what a writer says will not gain high marks.

Agreed action points

Sam will:

- Obtain a copy of the library's guide to referencing and learn how to apply the Harvard Referencing System.

- Manually review the education journals held by the library and identify those which are relevant to the research.

- Undertake a range of electronic searches using the British Education Index and Google Scholar and refine searches using a variety of key words.

The literature review

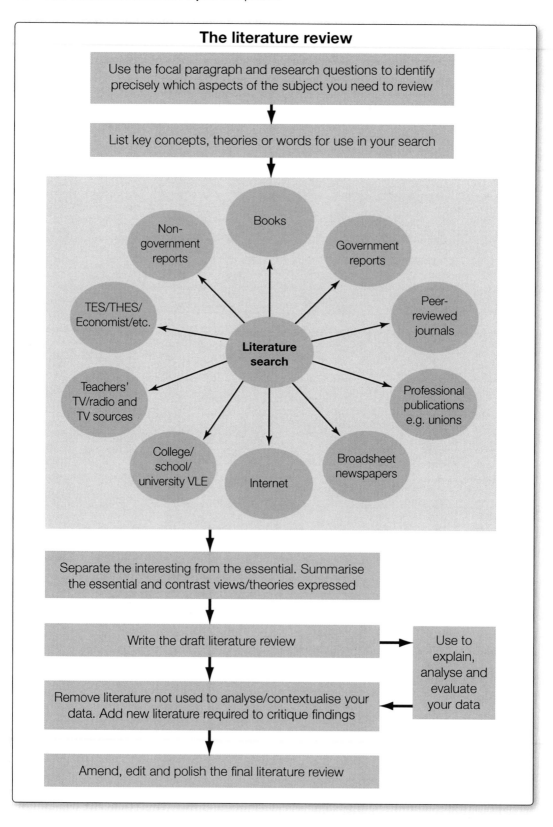

Use the focal paragraph and research questions to identify precisely which aspects of the subject you need to review

List key concepts, theories or words for use in your search

Books

Non-government reports

Government reports

TES/THES/Economist/etc.

Peer-reviewed journals

Literature search

Teachers' TV/radio and TV sources

Professional publications e.g. unions

College/school/university VLE

Internet

Broadsheet newspapers

Separate the interesting from the essential. Summarise the essential and contrast views/theories expressed

Write the draft literature review

Use to explain, analyse and evaluate your data

Remove literature not used to analyse/contextualise your data. Add new literature required to critique findings

Amend, edit and polish the final literature review

Handout 3.1

SOURCES OF LITERATURE IN ORDER OF ACADEMIC CREDIBILITY

- Peer-reviewed journals with an international reputation.

- Peer-reviewed journals with a national reputation.

- Seminal books by authors with a high academic reputation.

- Books by authors with a high academic reputation.

- Acts of Parliament, White Papers, Green Papers, Government reports, reports and papers from local government and quasi-autonomous governmental organisations (QUANGOS), e.g. Ofsted. Note that these reports, while important, are not unbiased.

- Professional journals, including publications by professional bodies, trade unions and employer organisations.

- Quality press publications such as *The Times Educational Supplement, The Times Higher Education, The Economist, The Spectator.*

- The broadsheet newspapers, including *The Times, Guardian, Independent* and *Telegraph.*

- TV and radio quality documentaries and Teachers TV.

- You will note that no mention has been made of the Internet. This is because websites range in academic quality from the highly respectable and influential to absolute dross. When using websites it is imperative that you critically evaluate the provenance of the site. For example, who funds and runs the site, what is its editorial policy and how often is the material on it updated?

CHOOSING YOUR RESEARCH METHODOLOGY

Aim of tutorial

To help you decide which research methodology, quantitative or qualitative, is most suitable for your research. To achieve this, both methodologies are defined and evaluated. Additionally, other aspects of methodology such as ethics, triangulation, validity and reliability are explored.

Areas covered in this tutorial

Sam's reflection

25 October

*Richard said that we were going to talk about research methodology today and review what is meant by the terms generalisability, ethics, validity, **reliability**, **sampling**, **triangulation** and bias. It all sounds very technical to me and I'm not sure that I see the point of it. I mean, I can see why I need to be able to design and use questionnaires and interview schedules, but what's the point of delving into the detail of the research process? I really don't want to go to tonight's session. Between this course and problems at work I'm shattered. But I suppose I must.*

Review of tutorial

'Hi Sam.'

'Hello,' I said, feeling jaded and tired.

'That's rather half-hearted. I thought that you'd be up for this one.'

'Well, we have an inspection at work and the dog didn't look too well this morning, so I . . .'

'Thought wouldn't it be nice to have the night off.'

'I admit that I did think about cancelling the session.'

'I'm glad that you didn't. Choosing the correct research methodology is a very important part of the research process. Anyway, I told my partner that I would be late for our salsa lesson tonight because I was seeing you. You can't imagine the grief I got. So it's a good job you're here.'

I hadn't really thought about the impact that cancelling at short notice might have on Richard and I felt glad that I had made the effort to attend.

Two approaches to education research – quantitative and qualitative

'Today we're going to look at quantitative and qualitative approaches to research. All of the key texts that I have highlighted on my Recommended reading list cover this area. So dip into the book that you feel most comfortable with to supplement and challenge what I say. These two methodologies are often represented as opposing **paradigms**, with qualitative research exploring people's attitudes, beliefs, feelings and perceptions and quantitative research concerned with numbers, quantities and observable facts. But this oppositional view isn't very helpful. The truth is, most research contains elements of both approaches and you should read Richard Pring's (2004) excellent article on the *False Dualism of Education Research*, in which he argues against this idea.'

'OK, but in simple terms what are the differences between the two approaches?'

Quantitative research

'There are several and the easiest way for me to explain them is to pose them as a series of opposites. Cohen et al. (2011) suggest that very often the purpose of quantitative research is to test a theory or verify a claim. This may involve carrying out controlled experiments, counting or measuring some phenomena such as exam results, or collecting data from statistical records, detailed observations, questionnaires or experiments. The idea is to be as objective as possible. To achieve this, the researcher tries to minimise any effect that their own beliefs, values and opinions might have on the data. They remain detached from the research participants and the data they collect from them. The nature of the data they're interested in is hard, impersonal and factual and they seek to generalise their findings across time and beyond the location in which they collect the data. We'll talk about how to analyse quantitative data in a later tutorial. (➡ *Tutorial 9)*

Ask a silly question and get a complex answer, I thought. There was a lot to take in but I decided to stay quiet and hear what he had to say about qualitative data.

Qualitative research

'On the other hand Cohen et al. (2011) say that the purpose of qualitative research is to generate theories not to verify them. It is concerned with discovery rather than proof and the researcher attempts to collect data without interfering with the normal flow of life. Data can be collected using observations, interviews, questionnaires and focus groups and will describe attitudes, beliefs and feelings. However, the nature of the data means it isn't possible to accurately measure the phenomena under review. The values of the researcher and the relationship they have with the respondents also affect how the data are interpreted. Effectively, the researcher uses their own knowledge, experience and understanding to make sense of it (Denscombe 2010). The nature of the data in which qualitative researchers are interested will be complex, impressionistic, personal, soft and rich and it's impossible to communicate this adequately using numbers. The findings won't be generalisable but they will be relatable to similar situations and of interest to people in what might appear quite different settings (Cohen et al. 2011). We'll talk about the presentation and analysis of qualitative data in a future tutorial. (➡ *Tutorial 8*)

'Why would people in different settings be interested?'

'Qualitative research is concerned with people and, while the setting may change, human nature stays the same. So, although there will be differences, many of the same issues will be present in most settings. If you don't believe me about human nature read "Meditations" by the Roman Emperor, Marcus Aurelius.'

'Marcus Aurelius? Wasn't he in *Gladiator*?' I said, waiting for Richard to take the bait. Instead he just gave me a pitying look, his eyes turned towards heaven. I moved quickly on. 'From what you say it sounds as if my research is going to be qualitative.'

Mixing research methodologies

'I think it is fair to say that your work is broadly qualitative but it would be possible to fine-tune it and include an element of quantitative research.'

'OK,' I said doubtfully.

Richard smiled and continued. 'Don't look so worried. I'm sure you can cope with a few numbers.'

'But I don't have any numbers to analyse. I'm dealing solely with words. Why go out of my way to manufacture quantitative data?'

'There are several dimensions to doing a project like this, one of which is to develop your skills as a researcher. My old Dad used to say "If the only tool you have in your bag is a hammer then every problem you see will look like a nail".

We aim to provide you with a full toolkit. Only when you know the value of quantitative data and how to collect, analyse and use it will you be in a position to say with confidence that you don't require it.'

'OK,' I said, 'but I still can't see what useful quantitative data I could collect.'

'You intend to use questionnaires with some teachers? What sort of questions do you intend to ask?'

'I was going to use some **Likert**-style questions and ask them to say on a scale of one to five how they felt about a series of statements.' (➡ *Tutorial 7*) As I spoke, I realised that I would have plenty of numbers to report. 'OK,' I said sheepishly, 'I've got numbers.'

Richard grinned. 'You have indeed. However, you should realise that what you would be doing is reporting qualitative data in a quantitative form because the rating given by the teachers for various statements is effectively just a descriptor of their qualitative feelings and perceptions. In addition, whenever you assess people's opinions, there will always be variation in how they interpret and understand the question you've asked. This is why caution is needed when analysing semi-quantitative data such as this. It can be like "castles built on sand"; there is the danger that you will make quantitative claims without adequate foundation.'

Sam's reflection

26 October

This was an eye-opener. I'd heard of quantitative and qualitative methodologies previously, but I thought that they were two completely separate approaches. Now I realise that my project is like a recipe. I can add in a taste of the quantitative if I want to.

It's probably too simplistic to say that qualitative research deals in words and quantitative research in numbers, but I think that's a simple way to describe the difference between them.

I wonder if my aversion to quantitative research is based on my fear of maths. I'm certainly more confident dealing with words but I shouldn't ➡

be worried about analysing numbers. After all, they're just statistics and that's only one step up from arithmetic. Is that me just whistling in the dark? No, be positive, there is a tutorial on analysing quantitative data (➡ *Tutorial 9*) later in the course and there is no reason why I can't master it. On that positive note I'm going to watch 'Game of Thrones' and go to bed. I wonder who's going to be bumped off tonight?

Review of tutorial

Generalisability vs relatability

'Now, linked to the choice of methodology are questions about generalisability, ethics, validity, reliability, triangulation and bias. Do you remember that we briefly mentioned them in Tutorial 2?'

'Yes,' I said uncertainly.

'Well, you need to write a paragraph or so on each of them in your methodology chapter. If you use the index in Denscombe (2010), you'll find that he defines these terms in very accessible ways. They are worth looking at and contrasting with what I'm about to say.'

'OK,' I said.

'Let's start with generalisability. As I said earlier, generalisability relates to how far your findings are applicable across the board. For example, if you were researching teaching methods in an inner city school in Birmingham, could you claim that your findings are applicable to all secondary schools in England?'

'No,' I said firmly. 'The issues faced by teachers in an inner city school in Birmingham are very different from those in a leafy suburb in Kent.'

'Exactly. They're not comparable. How might you make your research more comparable?'

I had to think about that but finally said, 'I could include different schools from different areas of the country.'

'You could. What you're suggesting is that you need a more representative sample. But is that practical given that you are a sole researcher with a deadline fast approaching?'

'No.'

'Correct. In general, qualitative findings tend to be unique to a particular time and place and to the people that took part in the research. Whereas the results from large-scale quantitative projects are very often generalisable because the sample selected is statistically representative of whatever group or population you are looking at. So, don't claim that your work is generalisable. Instead suggest that it is relatable.'

'As per Marcus Aurelius,' I suggested.

Richard just looked at me and shook his head.

Sam's reflection

27 October

I had assumed that to be any good my research would have to apply to all schools or at least a good number of them. It's a comfort to realise that it doesn't have to. I suppose this goes back to something Richard said at our first meeting: research at this level is about improving professional knowledge and/or practice. It's not about solving the problems of the world. So all I'm going to claim for my research is that it's relatable to schools similar to mine and that aspects of the research might be of interest to other schools. Maybe that's one reason to make sure that I disseminate my findings. My findings will be of particular interest to teachers in my school because the research is about our unique situation.

Review of tutorial

Ethics and research

'So what about ethical considerations?' I asked.

'Well, in addition to Denscombe have a look at the British Educational Research Association website **www.bera.ac.uk**. They publish a set of ethical guidelines that education researchers should follow. The main ones that you need to consider are: do no harm, obtain informed consent from all participants, respect participants' anonymity and abide by all legal requirements, including those of child protection and data protection. Now let's take each one of these in turn.'

I settled back in my chair and waited.

'You should never undertake research that can harm the participants physically, mentally or emotionally. That's why your project has to be approved before you can start to collect data. Unfortunately, it is not always possible to predict if a particular piece of research will upset or harm participants, so you need to be constantly on the lookout for any signs of distress, and if you notice any you must suspend your research.'

'I'm dealing with adult teachers so I don't suppose I'll have much of a problem. But if I do decide to ask the kids some questions, is there anything I need to watch out for in particular?'

'When dealing with children or vulnerable adults you need to be very careful as there are specific legal obligations. Under these circumstances, guardians or other responsible adults – in this case "responsible" is used in a legal sense and could mean social workers – need to be involved to ensure that no harm results from any research undertaken and that only **authentic data** are collected.'

'This sounds like a right minefield. How does any research get done in schools?'

'The general position is that permission from parents or guardians isn't necessary if the research is part of the researcher's normal professional role. So, gathering assessment data on pupils' work or the evaluation of lessons is usually acceptable. But it's vital to check with the head that these general permissions apply in your school. Parental permission is vital when photographs or video recordings are used. Some schools have a standard letter signed by parents for this, but you must check. You also need to ensure that you comply with the legal requirements for working with children and vulnerable adults; this usually means having the appropriate enhanced CRB check, which I assume you have.'

'Yes,' I said.

'But linked closely to the above discussion is the concept of informed consent. This is particularly difficult for teachers when they are researching their own pupils. For example, if you give your class a questionnaire to complete, they're likely to believe that they must complete it. How much free choice is there in that? You must explain to all your participants the nature and purpose of your research and emphasise that they are under no obligation to take part in the research and that they can withdraw from it at any stage.'

'That could cause a problem if at a later stage a group of children say they want to withdraw because I cancelled their visit to the theatre.'

'That's true, but you must give them that option and honour your commitment to them. That's why it's useful to think of what other sources of data from your everyday practice, such as children's work and assessment results, you could use. These are "authentic" too and less subject to bias.'

'What about **confidentiality** and anonymity?'

'Anonymity is certainly important. You must make it clear to participants that their identity will not be revealed . . .'

'Because they may not be as frank and honest with me if they think that they might be identified,' I suggested.

'Partly. What people say to you may harm them if their identity is revealed. For example, if a teacher criticises the head or board of governors. So, use pseudonyms such as "Teacher A" or "Pupil Alpha". But it's also about protecting their right to privacy. They may not want others to know how they feel about an issue, because they know they are in the minority. If you use common names such as Mohammed, Bill or Mary as a pseudonym, mention this in order to avoid any confusion. But even where you have used a pseudonym it's important that you don't reveal the person's identity by providing other information which enables the reader to identify the person. So, if the school has four maths teachers, three of whom are in their twenties, it will be obvious who you are speaking of if you say, "One maths teacher, who has worked at the school for over 20 years, said . . ."'

'What about data protection?' I asked.

Richard took a deep breath and said, 'That's a good example of a legal and an ethical requirement. You should only hold data necessary for the research and it must be disposed of in a secure way as soon as possible. Unlike the British

Secret Service, be particularly careful with data on laptops and memory sticks and don't lose them or leave them on the bus. You also need to securely shred all notes and transcripts written as part of the research.'

Sam's reflection

27 October

I thought that the ethical side was going to be a tick-box exercise. A case of 'going through the motions'. But I realise now that it's much more important than that. I have important responsibilities to the people taking part in my research and it's vital that they don't suffer in any way as a result. In addition, if things do go wrong I need to demonstrate that I acted responsibly at every stage of the process.

The 'normal professional role' bit was interesting. This seems to mean that I can carry out research in school if it's connected to my normal duties. I still need the Head's approval. But that's no bad thing, as it's important to get management's support for what I am doing and any changes that I might want to recommend.

It's occurred to me that Richard used the word 'authentic' data. He used it in passing but, knowing him, there's more to it than I think. 'Authentic' means 'real', 'genuine' or 'valid', which is what I want my data to be. After all, what's the point if my data doesn't bear some relation to the real situation?

Review of tutorial

Validity

'Now we need to discuss "validity". What do you think "validity" means?'

'Well, a valid opinion is one that is based on a good argument or evidence,' I ventured. 'So I assume that valid research is research which is based on firm foundations.'

'Very good. We just need to tweak it a bit because some terms have a slightly different meaning to the normal when used in a technical sense. In this case we're really talking about the validity of your approach. A "valid" approach is one that ensures that you actually measure what you intended to measure. This is why we make such a fuss about the research questions. (➡ *Tutorial 1*) When you say that you're measuring such things as "enjoyment", "motivation", or "engagement", you need to ensure that you use an approach that will actually measure these things. So, how would you measure "enjoyment"?'

'I'd ask the participants if they enjoyed the activity.'

'What does "enjoy" mean?'

'Now you're pulling my leg. I know what "enjoy" means and so do they.'

'But do they? This word means different things to different people; its interpretation is subjective. One person's enjoyment is another's greatest moment in their life. So you need to define "enjoyment" and be clear that the questions you ask relate to your definition.'

'Because then I would be measuring what I set out to measure.'

'Exactly! Of course some aspects of your approach will be more valid than others and the task here is to comment on which aspects are more or less valid and what could be done to improve validity. The important thing is that you demonstrate your understanding of the concept and explain how you dealt with it. Too often people write "my approach was valid because . . .". There are always aspects that are more valid than others.'

Reliability

Without pause Richard continued. 'Once you've covered validity you can look at its partner, reliability. Reliability is concerned with the question: to what extent would I get the same results if I were to repeat the research again?'

'I can see a problem with that right away. With a scientific experiment it's possible to get the same result time after time. But I can't interview the same person twice and expect exactly the same answers.'

'Good! That's another difference between quantitative and qualitative research. Very often in quantitative research you can repeat the research and get the same or very similar results whereas this is not possible in qualitative research.'

'So how do you ensure reliability in qualitative research?'

'It's a matter of transparency. You need to describe how you carried out your research in sufficient detail to enable others to repeat your work if they wish to. You provide what is known as an "**audit trail**". For example, you will need to explain how you drew up and tested your questionnaire, how you selected and approached your respondents and exactly how the questionnaire was administered and analysed. By providing this information the reader can make a judgement about how rigorous your research has been and how reasonable your interpretation of the data has been. They could even repeat your research if they wished to confirm or refute its findings.

Sam's reflection

28 October

Previously I wasn't too keen about revealing any weaknesses in my research. But I can now see why it is important to critically evaluate my approach. Only if I'm critical can I identify and address issues surrounding validity and reliability. So, I need to identify those aspects of my work that help validity and reliability and those that have detracted from it and suggest ways that I might improve them in the future.

Review of tutorial

Sampling

Something had been bubbling away at the back of my mind and finally I asked, 'Would the sample I select affect validity and reliability?'

'Yes, a random sample that was large enough to be statistically significant would help reliability. But the samples in most small-scale research projects are neither genuinely random nor sufficiently large to be statistically significant.'

'So what are the main types of samples that students use?'

'A few try to use a random sample. They give each person in the **population** that they want to sample a number and then select numbers at random. The problem is that humans are always looking for patterns so we are very poor at picking numbers at random.'

'What about putting the numbers in a hat?'

'Better, but not perfect. What they need to use is a random number generator – Excel has one.'

'That sounds complex. Why can't you just grab the people who are in the staff room and use them,' I said, expecting him to explode with indignation.

'What you're talking about is convenience sampling and it does have its place, but I wouldn't recommend that you use it because it's hard to justify and makes you look lazy and slapdash.'

'But sometimes the people in the staffroom are the very ones you want to speak to because they have specific information that you require,' I said, still trying to avoid using random sampling.

'Now you are talking about purposive sampling. That's where you choose certain people because they have the information you require.'

'I can pick who I want, can I?' I said, with surprise and relief.

'Indeed you can. In fact, it's probably the most used sampling technique for small-scale qualitative research.'

'Great. It sounds a lot better than convenience sampling.'

'Clearly you understand the value of "spin" in what you write. You'll make a Head one day,' Richard said, laughing. 'But it's also worth mentioning "stratified sampling". Any idea what that is?'

'Stratified means layered, so it probably means that I choose samples from different layers of the population.'

'In a sense, yes. Essentially you select subpopulations relevant to your study and take samples from those.'

'OK, so I could split the population into males and females and take a sample from each group or split the teachers by year group? Or I could divide the teaching staff into deputy heads, assistant heads, head of year, subject leaders, teachers and teaching asistants.'

'Exactly. If you want to look at sampling in more detail, Denscombe (2010) has a good section on it and I like Vic Barnett's (2002) book as well.'

Sam's reflection

29 October

So, sampling can be random, convenience, purpositive or stratified. But it must also be possible to combine two or more methods. For example, I could have three separate groups – say, senior managers, heads of year and teachers, and then use purposive sampling to select who I spoke to in each group. That's worth thinking about. I do like the idea of purposive sampling.

That said, Richard's Dad and his hammer is haunting me. I need to fully understand each sampling technique and how each might affect my results. Because only then will I be able to argue convincingly that the approach I used was best.

Review of tutorial

Triangulation

'We've covered a lot today, but there are a couple more things that need to be included in the methodology section. They are triangulation and bias.'

'Ah, I know about triangulation; it means that I should use two or more research methods.'

'That's partially correct. What you're trying to do is view the issue that you're researching from more than one viewpoint. Why do you think this is important?'

'It's about trying to see things from different angles?' I suggested.

'Exactly. If you look at an object from just one angle you only see one aspect or surface of it. If you look at it from a different angle, previously unseen features may come into focus.'

'So how can I achieve this rounded view?'

'Well, there are different types of triangulation. The ones which you might use include methodological triangulation. This involves the use of different methodologies such as quantitative and qualitative to get a fix on the situation. Using a mixed methodology approach you could compare and contrast what a teacher says in an interview (qualitative data) about improving performance with the schools SATS results from the last five years (quantitative data). In this way you're collecting data from two sources, each of which is underpinned by a different research methodology.'

'Would it matter if both methods were qualitative?'

'No it wouldn't, but then you would be using methods triangulation not methodological triangulation. For example, you might interview a group of teachers about the teaching methods that they use and compare this with your findings from a classroom observation. One method reveals what the teachers said they do and the second what they actually do. The two may well be the same but you would be surprised how often they differ.'

'So I don't need to use three methods to triangulate my data.'

'No it's a common misunderstanding that you have to use three methods to triangulate data. But think of the issue you are researching as one point of the triangle and your two data collection methods as the other two points.'

'I like the sound of methods triangulation. It sounds straightforward and doable,' I said.

'Many would agree with you. It's the most popular type of triangulation with students,' he said. 'But you might also want to consider data source triangulation. This is where you collect data on the same topic from different groups of participants. For example, in your assignment you could collect data from teachers and children. This would give you a more rounded picture of the issue.'

'I think I'll be looking at teachers in different year groups. Does that count?' I interjected.

'That's a good point and, yes, it does count. So you need to say that in your write-up. The fourth type of triangulation involves collecting data at different times or more than once from your participants. This allows you to pick up on any changes in what people have to say as a result of the passage of time and the development of their ideas. Fifthly, and much more unlikely, you can use more than one researcher to collect the data. But by its very nature it's not an approach that sole researchers can use.'

'Do I have to use each type of triangulation or can I rely on just one?'

'For most small-scale research projects you'll use only one or two approaches. The most common are methods triangulation and data source triangulation. If you use either of these approaches you gain a more complete picture of the issue that you are investigating and you improve the accuracy of the data collected. This improved accuracy also helps you to claim validity for your work, as you are measuring what you set out to measure from more than one standpoint.'

Sam's reflection

30 October

Triangulation is obviously important but I don't think that it is difficult to achieve. My research involves collecting data from teachers in different year groups and at different levels. So I will be able to claim an element of stratified sampling.

Then, if I interview the teachers and observe them teaching, I'll be able to claim methods triangulation because I will be confirming the accuracy or otherwise of what they said by observation of what they have done.'

Review of tutorial

Bias

'So that just leaves bias. I don't think that it will be much of a problem as I don't think that any of my participants have extreme views.'

'If only it were that easy. Bias is always present and it doesn't necessarily come from people with extreme views. The nature of qualitative research is that people's opinions are based on their whole life experience and will be affected by more than the issue under consideration. Even with quantitative research, bias is possible because particular samples are chosen or the data may be analysed in a way which favours a particular result.'

'I thought that bias was something that my participants would show. I didn't realise that I could be the source.'

'The researcher always influences the result . . .'

'And it's my task to evaluate the possible effect on my findings.'

'Correct. In the case of research when do you think that your bias surfaces for the first time?'

'When you start to write up your findings?' I suggested.

'I think it starts with your choice of topic.'

'If that's the case then you can never produce a piece of unbiased research. That can't be right.'

'In the case of scientific research where you're dealing with inanimate objects, it is easier to reduce bias to negligible levels. The researcher doesn't have an emotional or social relationship with the "**variables**" involved. But in the social sciences research bias starts with your choice of topic. What you choose to research says something about your own interests and what you think is important. Therefore, it's virtually impossible for the social science researcher to come to a topic without some prior knowledge or opinion about the issues involved. In all probability it's that prior knowledge which has attracted them to the topic. Effectively, it is not possible for the researcher to come to the research with "an empty mind". The best they can hope for is an "open mind".'

This sounded like one of those problems that had no real solution. But I tried anyway and asked, 'So how do I deal with bias in my research?'

'Firstly you need to recognise that whatever you write will contain an element of bias. Secondly, you need to demonstrate that you've attempted to counter your own bias by using a good range of writers in your literature review, some of whom you agree with and others you don't. Thirdly, when analysing the data look for alternative interpretations, especially if the findings confirm your own views. This is particularly important at Master's level. Very rarely does data have only one interpretation. Try to challenge your own interpretations. Fourthly, explain to the reader how you carried out your research, analysed your data and your thinking behind the key decisions that you made. This will enable them to judge for themselves to what extent your findings and interpretations are a reasonable representation of the situation.'

'It also helps me to claim reliability,' I interjected. 'It's all about telling the reader what you've done, how you did it and why you did it. It's about leaving an audit trail.'

'Exactly. That is a really good way to think about it. But it is also important to consider to what extent you are an "insider" or an "outsider".'

'I remember this. I'm an insider because I'm researching teachers in my place-ment and that will affect how they see and respond to me. They may give me the answer that they think I want to hear.' (➡ *Tutorial 1*)

'True, but of course if you were an outsider – possibly a researcher working for the local authority – the same problems might arise. This is really about the role of the researcher. It's difficult, but you need to consider how your relationship with others in your study could influence the result. Here, have a look at this handout on insider and outsider research (➡ *Handout 4.1*) and read Hockey's (1993) origi-nal article on the subject. Now, lastly, let's look at working at Master's level.'

Working at Master's level: Ontology

'OK. At Master's level you have to explain your philosophical approach to research. This handout will help you to get to grips with the terminology (➡ *Handout 4.2 below*). The first issue you need to talk about is your **ontology**. If you believe, as scientists do, that there is only one reality and it is the job of researchers to discover that reality, you would be described as a realist. But if you believe that reality is at least partially constructed by each individual person then you are a nominalist. Effectively, your ontology describes how you view the social world.'

'But we do all live in the same reality, so how can people create their own reality. I mean Britain and America do exist. That's reality.'

'Fair point. But can you see that a woman's experience of living in, say, London would be different from a man's. They may both travel to work on the Tube, do the same job and go out and socialise, etc. But they have different experience and may react very differently to similar experiences. In the end each will view London through the lens of their own unique experiences and this becomes their reality.'

'So it's not that we have diametrically opposed views of reality; it's just that we perceive certain issues differently and the sum of these differences creates "our reality"?'

Working at Master's level: Epistemology

'That's about it. Now **epistemology** is about knowledge and what constitutes knowledge. If you are a subjectivist, then your ontology will be nominalist and you will be an anti-positivist. You will accept people's opinions, views, attitudes and beliefs as valid knowledge and as something worth collecting and exploring. However, if your ontology is realist you would consider such knowledge as useless. As a positivist you would only be interested in facts and figures – stuff that can be transmitted in tangible form. Positivists believe in the scientific approach to knowledge – knowledge has to be testable, and the results obtained from a single experiment must be repeatable for the finding to be valid.

'So I'm betting that if I'm using qualitative research, I'm an anti-positivist.'

'Correct, but there is one more stage you need to go through before you reach your methodology. If you are an anti-positivist then you will probably use an **interpretivist** methodology. Now, interpretivist research is a paradigm within which various research methodologies sit.'

'Remind me, what's a paradigm?'

'It's a construction. A sort of high-level way of thinking. So, capitalism and communism are different ways of thinking about how the world should be governed and they are competing paradigms.'

'So what are the methodologies that sit in the interpretivist paradigm?'

'Well, you have qualitative, phenomenological, grounded theory, ethnographic, emancipatory ...'.

'Enough,' I cried. 'And I suppose they are all different?'

'Yes, but they do share certain characteristics. For example, they all believe that the individual has at least some control over their lives and they are ideographic in that they focus on the lived experiences of individuals. Compare that with the positivists who believe that individuals are controlled to a considerable extent by social structures, relations and rules. In other words, people live in a deterministic world. So it follows that they think it is necessary to look at large groups of people, not individuals, if they are to discover the single reality that is the social world.'

'My head's hurting on this. Where can I go to read up on this?'

'First look at the handout I've just given you. Then have a look at the first chapter of Cohen et al. (2011). You'll probably have to read it more than once to understand it, but it's worth the effort as it can open your mind to some really important issues about how we perceive reality. I also like Pring's (2004) *Philosophy of Educational Research*. He writes beautifully and is always clear. But perhaps the fullest treatment of these issues that relate to your research can be found in Crotty (1998). If you should get interested in the subject, have a read of Trigg (2001). Now, I suggest you go away and do a bit of reading in this area and we'll pick it up again at our next session. But please remember I have talked about these two philosophical approaches as if they are committed enemies. You need to go back and read what Pring (2004) said about the false dualism of research.'

'OK. But I think you have managed to put me off doing my research project at Master's level.'

'Don't be like that. This is a fascinating area and, once you have mastered the jargon, you will quickly see that it's not as difficult as you might think. As I say, we will discuss it again. But for now I need to get to that salsa lesson or I'll be in trouble.'

Sam's reflection

31 October

Welcome to the world of paranoia. From what Richard says it seems that everything I say, write and think is drenched in bias. How am I supposed to get around that? I suppose what I need to do is to think carefully about what I write and try and understand why I've interpreted the data the way I have. Sometimes what I think will be entirely reasonable – such as hating marking. That's just normal, a part of every teacher's DNA. Isn't it?

But I do need to challenge my views and opinions, test them against the evidence and see what other points of view are valid. Then I need to make sure that they are fairly represented in my work. Hang on – a ping moment has just occurred – if I end up with an interpretation of the data that is unexpected or which I don't like that's probably a good sign, or is it?

The *stuff on ontology, epistemology and interpretivism was difficult. I need to listen agin to the recording and do some reading. I'll start with Cohen, Manion and Morrissey and then have a look at Crotty. I need to identify anything I don't understand and ask Richard about it when we next meet.*

Record of tutorial

Student: Sam Sylon   **Date: 25/10/XX**

SUMMARY OF KEY LEARNING POINTS

- Qualitative approaches are about subjective attitudes and beliefs. The unit of analysis is words and while the responses are unique to the location in which they were collected, the findings may be relatable to similar situations.

- Quantitative approaches are objective and are often about measurement of phenomena. The unit of analysis is numbers. Findings may be generalisable depending on how representative the sample was.

- Quantitative and qualitative approaches can be combined.

- Care needs to be taken when making quantitative judgements from qualitative data.

- Key ethical issues are: do no harm, protect the participants' well-being and maintain their anonymity. This is particularly important when dealing with children and vulnerable adults. Obtain genuine informed consent from all participants and ensure that they understand their right to withdraw at any stage. Obtain permission from all stakeholders prior to starting the research and observe all data protection requirements.

- Validity is concerned with ensuring that the data collection methods used actually measure or describe the phenomena the researcher is interested in. ➡

- In quantitative research reliability relates to what extent the data collection methods used would give the same or similar results if repeated. In qualitative research reliability is concerned with the reasonableness of the approach adopted and the decisions made by the researcher.

- Sampling may be random, purposive, convenience, stratified, or a combination of these.

- Triangulation means looking at the data from more than one angle. There are different types of triangulation including: methodological, methods, data source, time delay and multiple researcher.

- Bias is always present because people are involved in research. Bias can result from participants or researchers.

- At Master's level you are required to discuss your ontological and epistemological stance. The key decision you have to make is: are you a realist – believing that there is only one reality and your job as a researcher is to find it? Or are you a nominalist who thinks that people play a part in creating the reality that they live in? From that decision will flow your research stance.

Agreed action points

Sam will:

- Review the final list of research questions and determine which research methodology is most suitable to use and why.

- Obtain and read a copy of the BERA ethical guidelines from www.bera. ac.uk.

- Identify which sampling method to use.

- Consider how to deal with ethics validity, reliability, triangulation and bias when designing the research programme.

- Read around the issues associated with ontology and epistemology and prepare a list of specific questions you want to ask at the next meeting.

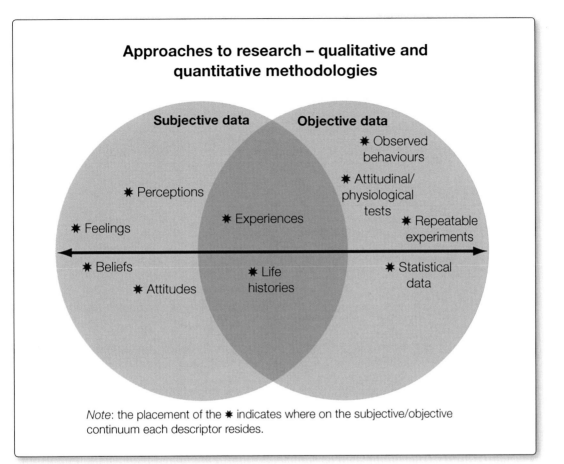

Approaches to research – qualitative and quantitative methodologies

Subjective data

Objective data

✳ Perceptions

✳ Feelings

✳ Experiences

✳ Observed behaviours

✳ Attitudinal/ physiological tests

✳ Repeatable experiments

✳ Beliefs

✳ Attitudes

✳ Life histories

✳ Statistical data

Note: the placement of the ✳ indicates where on the subjective/objective continuum each descriptor resides.

Handout 4.1

RESEARCHING IN FAMILIAR SETTINGS – STRENGTHS AND WEAKNESSES

Strengths	Weaknesses
Familiarity with the setting may mean that the researcher isn't surprised by what they see.	Familiarity with the setting means that the researcher may not challenge his/her own assumptions about the organisation.
The researcher blends into the background and is accepted by the respondents, so suspicion may be less.	The researcher's new role may be challenged by participants.
The researcher may already have a good relationship with participants.	The power and professional relationships between the researcher and the respondent may become unclear during the research process.
The researcher's prior knowledge can help identify the most pertinent issues in the organisation.	Knowledge of the setting can lead to the researcher ignoring everyday events and practices.
It's easier for the researcher to access people and places.	The organisation's management may influence the researcher's actions and thinking.
The researcher may be more trusted by the participants.	The researcher may be judged by staff as a result of prior knowledge and there may be an impact on future relationships.
The researcher is in a better position to judge whether participants are likely to respond accurately.	The researcher may think that the participants share his/her views and this may bias the analysis of findings.
Researcher possesses a great deal of insider knowledge that can assist the research.	The researcher may not be aware of or may be misguided about relevant issues in the organisation.
	Anonymity may be a significant ethical issue as the researcher may know the participants.
	The participants may not take the researcher/research seriously and instead engage in 'game playing'.
(After Hockey 1993; Robson 2011).	

Handout 4.2

APPROACHES TO KNOWLEDGE

	Subjectivist approach	Objectivist approach
Ontology	Reality and truth are, at least in part, the product of individual perception – **Nominalist**. It is the researcher's job to understand how these realities differ between people.	Reality and truth are a given and are external to the individual – **Realist**. It is the researcher's job to uncover this single reality.
Epistemology	Knowledge is subjective and is based on experience and insight – **Anti-Positivist** and is normally researched using an **Interpretive** methodology such as qualitative research.	Knowledge is hard, real, single and unchanging and is capable of being transmitted in a tangible form – **Positivist**. Such knowledge is sought using a Qualitative/Scientific methodology
Human nature	Human beings are creative and exercise choice – **Agency**. They are able to exercise control over their life and work, to take responsibility and make meaningful decisions – **Voluntarist**. Therefore, an **Ideographic** approach is adopted by the researcher which is concerned with the views of individuals.	The external environment has a deterministic effect on human beings. External powers control and determine the individual's life and work – **Deterministic**. Therefore a **Nomothetic** approach is adopted by the researcher who is concerned with the actions/beliefs of large groups.

RESEARCH STRATEGIES – CASE STUDIES, ACTION RESEARCH AND SURVEYS

Aim of tutorial

To enable you to select the most appropriate strategy for your research.
To achieve this, each strategy is defined and evaluated.

Areas covered in this tutorial

Sam's reflection

5 November

Today we're looking at research strategies. I'm not entirely sure how these fit into the scheme of things. We've already discussed methodology which covered quantitative versus qualitative approaches and issues such as validity and reliability. And I know that in the future we'll be looking at data collection methods, so I wonder how research strategies differ from these.

Richard said that we would discuss various strategies including **case studies**, **action research** and **survey**. So what do I know about these terms? I've come across the word 'case' as in a legal case or a social worker's case. Both of these 'cases' focus on a single person and from working with social workers I know that these files are very detailed. So for a case study I would probably have to say who was involved, what they did and what were the sources of evidence that I used.

Action research sounds as if some action is taken and the researcher then describes what took place. But who does the action, the researcher or the people involved in the research? I think it's probably the researcher.

Surveys seem simpler. These would be about canvassing people's opinion. And most surveys only collect data from a sample of people don't they? I'm not sure if this is always the case – I'd better check. I wonder if these are the only strategies that researchers can use? I finish work early today. I'll pop into the library before tonight's session and see what other strategies are available.

Review of tutorial

Research terminology – a movable feast

I arrived early, excited by what I'd found in the library. Richard waved me into a chair.

'How are things?' he asked.

'Fine,' I said, 'I've got loads of questions.'

'That's good. It's always valuable when people prepare for the tutorial in advance. That way they can set the agenda and drive the discussion in the direction that meets their needs. So fire away.'

'You said that we would discuss three research strategies today. Case studies, action research and surveys. But I've been looking in the library and different authors refer to these as methodologies or methods and I've not found any that describe them as strategies, so I'm confused?'

'Welcome to the debate on research. One of the odd things about research is that, for a process which demands precision and detail, there is precious little agreement on the definitions for many of the terms commonly used. Some writers talk about case studies as a research method and describe qualitative or quantitative research as an approach to research rather than a methodology. What I try to do in these tutorials is simplify the discussion and just have four levels which students can easily understand. At the top level you have the broad philosophical and conceptual issues such as what is the nature of the research. Is your research based on a positivist or anti-positivist philosophy? When I talk about quantitative or qualitative approaches to research and how I know that what I am reporting has validity and is reliable, I call that my research methodology. Basically the methodology is concerned with the overarching principles and the structure of the research. But that's pretty vague so it needs shaping (➡ *Tutorial 4*). To do this I use the term 'research strategies', such as the case study, action research and survey that we'll discuss today. These strategies help me to organise and structure the research; to delineate the boundaries of the research and maintain control over the project. And finally I have research methods which are the tools I use to collect the data such as interviews and questionnaires. My approach is basically a four-stage process which involves identifying your research philosophy (ontology and epistemology) to the paradigm in which your research is set (scientific/quantitative or interpretive/

qualitative) to your research strategy (which framework are you going to use to organise your research – case study, surveys, etc.) to the practical (what data collection methods are you going to use?).'

The range of approaches available

'OK,' I said, a little uncertainly, still unsure that I fully understood. Undaunted I asked: 'But aren't there more strategies than just the three you've listed? I've just been reading about **ethnography**, for example.'

'Good question. There's a whole range of different strategies available and it's important to choose the most appropriate one for your research. It's almost certain that you could justify using several different ones. But the vast majority of small-scale educational research projects or dissertations at Level 6 are covered by case studies, action research and surveys. These are conceptually straightforward, easy to grasp and flexible enough to address a range of research questions. It's also the case that action research has become the method of choice to support professional development in professions such as teaching, nursing and social work. As for ethnography, while it is an interesting and valuable approach it's not an approach I'd recommend for undergraduates or even for many Master's level students.'

'Why not?'

'It involves collecting a huge amount of data and producing a highly detailed picture of the phenomena under review.'

'So we won't be talking about ethnographies?'

'We can come back to them later when we talk about Master's level studies.'

Sam's reflection

6 November

OK, I need to get this clear in my head. There are four levels to the research process that I have to cover. These are my:

- philosophical approach
- methodological approach

- *research strategy*
- *data collection methods.*

I suppose I could liken it to management in my school. The board of governors and head set out the vision and ethos. That's the philosophy. The governors, head and senior management team establish the approach the school will use to achieve its vision. That's the methodology. The head and senior management team work out the best way to deliver the vision. That's the strategy. And teachers select the right tools to get the job done. That's the methods. It's not a perfect analogy but it will do for now.

Review of tutorial

Case studies

'So, what's a case study?' asked Richard.

'I've been thinking about this. I think it's a detailed study of a person or event.'

'Not bad. They may certainly be about people and events but they can also be about phenomena: dyslexia, for example.'

'Or a particular change to the National Curriculum.'

'Indeed. As Yin (2009), Thomas (2010) and others describe it, a case study is the exploration of a bounded **instance** using multiple data collection methods which results in a highly detailed picture of the person, place or thing under examination. And it may involve some element of observation.'

'What do you mean by bounded?'

'Well, it would be possible to look at the reaction of one person to an issue, a small group, a large group or the entire population of the country. As a researcher you have to find some way to limit the size of your enquiry . . .'

'Because as a single researcher I have limited time and words to play with and, if I tried to collect data from too many people, I wouldn't have the space to report it in great detail. Which was what we were doing when we discussed the focus of my research' (➡ *Tutorial 1*).

'Precisely. So what boundaries might you set for a case study?'

Bounding my case study

'Boundaries? You mean limits?'

'Yes, though "**boundary**" is the correct term to use.' I said nothing and Richard continued, 'You could just look at one person, one class, one year group or just boys. So are you doing a case study?'

'Maybe,' I said doubtfully.

'Be careful. Are you going to use multiple data collection methods?'

'Well, I'm going to use questionnaires and interviews. Would that count as multiple methods?'

'Your instance is teaching methods. So you can certainly send a questionnaire to a number of teachers and interview a smaller number to get the detail necessary to build a picture of their perceptions. But, as many commentators argue, including Cohen, Mannion and Morrison (2011) and Hitchcock and Hughes (1995), to describe a situation in depth you will almost certainly have to undertake some observations. To be able to report the findings from three data collection tools you will probably have to focus on teaching methods used with one year group rather than all pupils aged 11–14.'

'Because I wouldn't have the space to write a detailed account of such a large group?''

'Exactly! You would need to bound your study to manageable proportions.'

Researching an 'instance'

'OK. So what exactly do you mean by instance?'

'It's as I said, the subject of a case study can be a person, a group of people, a process or an event. Indeed it can be just about any phenomenon that has a discernible identity which marks it out as separate.'

'We're back to a boundary again. Are there any criteria I can use to help me select and define an instance?'

'There are many, but some common ones are an instance which is particularly interesting or atypical, such as a group of pupils who don't speak English at home. Or a unique event such as an educational exchange between schools. And let's not forget that extreme instances can be interesting . . .'

'Like looking at the most or least able pupils in a class?'

'Yes, that's a particularly common choice. But so too is the situation where your boss asks you to look at a particular issue which you can then construct as a case study. Of course, one problem with case studies is that it's very unlikely that you'll find examples of the same case study in the literature because it is unique to your situation and for that reason your findings won't be generalisable to other situations.' (➡ *Tutorial 4*)

Case studies – generalisability vs relatability

'But it might be relatable?'

'True. What you want to do is to derive descriptions from the study that can be related to similar circumstances. How might "other circumstances" be similar?'

'They could have happened at the same time, in similar places or organisations or with a similar group of people.'

'Or under similar circumstances. Excellent. So going back to the example of a case study that looks at a school exchange, while you might be unable to find an evaluation of an exchange with say a school in Ljubljana, you would certainly find information on the impact of educational exchanges. Equally, other schools in the area may have had exchanges with other countries, so your experiences would still interest them. Before we move on can you suggest some advantages and disadvantages of the case study strategy?'

Advantages and disadvantages of case studies

'I suppose advantages would be things like the use of different methods and sources of data as they would help triangulation and validity. I can also make the project doable by setting sensible boundaries and I would be looking at something distinct and original. It also seems like a natural approach as I'm not changing anything. I'm just looking at what's there,'

'And disadvantages?'

'You've said that I can't generalise. … I'm struggling a bit,' I said honestly.

'Fair enough. Always remember that advantages can also be seen as disadvantage. If you're setting the boundaries . . .'

'Then I could introduce bias,' I said. 'Because, although I'm not intervening in what's going on, I may still influence the outcome in some way, particularly if I know the people involved. And I may end up wasting precious time collecting too much data from my multiple data collection methods.'

Sam's reflection

10 November

If I reduced the year groups covered by my research, then the case study strategy would be suitable for my project. It would give me the opportunity to use several different methods and get a much more detailed picture of what's going on. But, against that, my research will only represent the views of some of the teachers. What do I want? A small detailed picture or a large sketch of what is going on? I'm not sure. I really need to think about what I want to get out of the research and how useful it will be to the teachers and the school. Best to go back to my research questions I think.

Review of tutorial

Action research

'So what do you think action research is about then?'

'Action implies doing something. Evaluation is important in research, so something is done and it's then evaluated. I'm not sure who undertakes the action. The researcher or someone else?'

'OK. Let's flesh that out a bit. There are a number of different interpretations of the action **research strategy**. The term was first used by Kurt Lewin. He was an American academic and the context was very much about exploring strategies for social change and the principle was one of planning and implementing a social change followed by evaluation. However, the "British tradition" is one of practice or practitioner-based research with the goal of self-improvement.'

'That seems a bit self-centred. Surely professionals would want to have a positive impact on others in some way?'

'Action research practitioners are encouraged to share their findings with other professionals. This sharing of good practices spreads out like ripples on a pond and has a positive impact on others. Indeed, the core of action research is that it's a social process which involves the community. Your use of the word "impact" is important, though. One of the key criteria for using action research as a model for professional development is that it has an impact on practice. In your case the teaching habits of a group of teachers. To ensure that your final results are valid you have to undertake rigorous self-evaluation throughout the project. It's essential that this critical evaluation be ongoing throughout the research process and not just something you do at the end of the project.'

Models of action research

'But how do you actually do it?' I asked, feeling that I still had no clear idea of what action research was.

'There's a very good book by Koshy (2009) that you can take a look at, and Denscombe (2010) has a chapter on it that's very user friendly. Basically, action research is a cyclical process that starts with identifying a problem. Say you want to improve boys' achievement in reading. You might benchmark the existing position by collecting assessment scores and recording your own evaluations of the boys' standard of reading. You then collect data from the children and other teachers using interviews, observations or questionnaires to try to identify the problems. This is called **baseline data**. You reflect on the data collected and design a series of changes or **interventions** in how boys are taught to read in your target group. You then implement a single small change, monitor it and assess what impact it had. Only then do you implement another change. You keep going through this cycle until you are satisfied with the boys' level of achievement.'

'It sounds like a reflective diary would be very useful,' I said.

'Essential. What did you do? How did you do it? What effect did it have and how will you change the situation or process to make it better? I've seen some reflective diaries that have clearly been typed at the end of the project. They're almost useless. I've also seen fantastic examples where people have taken the "scrapbook" approach and included diagrams, mind maps, examples of pupils' work to illustrate points, news items. Great work.'

'I remember someone at work doing an action research project. They implemented a new maths package and evaluated it by collecting pupils' work. I don't recall what else they changed, if anything, and I don't think they kept a research diary. So was that action research? It sounds more like a case study to me!'

'I was hoping that you wouldn't ask that question! The accepted model is one where the practitioner implements an intervention, but subjects it to ongoing modification as a result of constantly evaluating the evidence. But remember that research methods are evolving; they're dynamic and people's understanding of them changes. A more recent version is that baseline evidence is gathered which describes the situation as it is. A single large-scale intervention is designed in the light of this evidence and implemented and the changes that result from this action are evaluated and reported. There is very little ongoing evaluation in this process and frankly the sponsors of this type of research aren't too bothered. What they want to see is an improvement in the situation.'

'I suppose that the impact is the most important thing, however it's been achieved,' I said.

'That's true, but the professional learning that takes place is also very important. You really want evidence that the practitioner has learnt something from the process and that this will influence and inform his/her future behaviour.'

'I can see that this is a touchy subject.'

'Not really, but there are competing agendas. It's OK to adopt the new approach which is comprised of just a single intervention. That's fine. But, you need to explain why you have done this rather than use the traditional cyclical approach in your research methodology chapter.'

Undertaking action research

'OK, so how should I carry out an action research project?'

'Certainly plan to keep a research diary and expect to modify your approach as a result of your observations. Begin by collecting "baseline" data of the status quo. Use the baseline data to justify your intervention. What is the target group, what are their needs as evidenced from diverse sources such as the levels of their work, colleagues' opinions, classroom observations by you and others? Remember the importance of authenticity in your data. Don't forget the conceptual framework and use evidence from diverse literature such as self-evaluation documents, Ofsted reports, subject association literature and government reports to inform your planned intervention. Then design and implement your change.'

'And what if it doesn't work?' I asked.

'Be prepared to change or abandon your intervention. It's just the same as with your teaching. If you find that a particular teaching method or resource isn't working, you don't continue to use it regardless of outcomes. You change it in some way in order to meet your needs.'

'It strikes me that a research report based on action research could look quite different from some of the others. Where does all this information go?'

'Sometimes a portfolio approach is possible, though this can be very time-consuming and it isn't always good preparation for writing up more formal projects. The literature review still applies as a means to summarise your reading. The methodology is relevant as you need to explain your understanding of action research and how it was implemented, including the intervention. Of course aspects such as validity, reliability, triangulation and ethics will always apply. In fact, there can be more ethical implications, as you will be very closely involved with the participants. The findings section may be slightly different in that you would present your baseline evidence, explain how this may have influenced your intervention and then present and evaluate the evidence of impact. This is where you could introduce evidence from your reflective diary if appropriate.'

'So it's a movable feast in many ways?'

'Not exactly, but try not to be too dogmatic. Explain and justify your strategy and be prepared to critique it in terms of other strategies such as case study and survey. The critical thing is that you justify the strategy you use in terms of the research objectives and, above all, try to be critical of accepted definitions and how your project relates to these. Also, try to ensure that you collect evidence of impact as this is the main purpose of action research and what managers and funding bodies want to see.'

'But how can I be sure that it was my intervention that caused the improvement observed and not something else?' I asked.

'You can't. Without a control group, this is very difficult to establish. However, you can compare achievement by current groups with that of similar groups before the intervention. If in the longer term raised achievement is sustained when the intervention continues, then you move closer to establishing that **causal relationship**.'

'It all sounds exciting and highly relevant to my practice, so I can appreciate its attractiveness. I think I could also sell it to my employer, which is useful because they don't always see the relevance of my studies to work and are reluctant to pay my course fees. So what about the advantages and disadvantages of action research?'

Advantages and disadvantages of action research

'I was afraid you were going to ask. The advantages would include a close relevance to practice, stakeholders and the researcher. Diverse evidence can be included, so that helps validity and triangulation, and the evidence is likely to be authentic in the sense that it often comes from pupils and colleagues.'

'And the disadvantages?'

'It's difficult to know for certain if your intervention has caused any change identified. It may just be that you're working harder as the teacher. The approach seems to be evolving and is a bit controversial. There also seems to be a focus on data collection and evaluation, rather than data analysis.'

Sam's reflection

14 November

I'm excited by the idea of action research. For the first time I can see a strong relevance to my practice, my institution and to my own professional development. But I'm worried that it could be difficult to comply with the accepted action research approach. This could leave me open to criticism, but Richard told me not to worry about that and to have the confidence to justify my approach and be prepared to critique it in the light of accepted models, so maybe the advantages outweigh the disadvantages. Unfortunately it is not an approach that I can use for this piece of research. I won't be implementing any change, just collecting and analysing what children think and feel. Mind you, the data collected might suggest possible interventions that I could make in the future. Now that's an idea.

Review of tutorial

Surveys

'So that leaves us with . . . ?'

'Surveys,' I said.

'Exactly. Did you look at Barnett (2002) for what he had to say on samples?'

'Not yet,' I said.

'Well, double up and see what he says about surveys more generally. But, based on your existing knowledge, what's a survey?'

'A survey involves collecting data from a large number of people in the hope that you can identify what is going on. Data can be collected from either the entire population or a sample of them and you'd usually collect the data at a single point in time.'

'What sampling techniques could you use?'

Richard was testing me but I remembered what he'd said in the last tutorial.

'I could use random sampling, stratified sampling or most likely purposive sampling and if I used convenience sampling I'd call it something else!' (➡ *Tutorial 4*)

'That's pretty good,' Richard said with a smile, 'but try to be a little less honest with your answers. So, what data collection tools could you use on your sample?'

Data collection tools used in surveys

'I could use questionnaires, interviews or focus groups.'

'You could also undertake observations. We'll talk more about questionnaires, interviews and observations in a later tutorial (➡ *Tutorials 6 and 7*), but what are your initial thoughts on these methods?'

'Questionnaires are useful for larger samples and can be structured for easy analysis and they're straightforward to administer.'

'What about bias?'

'It's probably minimised because the researcher has less influence on the participants. Although the questions you ask could be biased and push participants towards a certain answer.'

'And interviews?'

'Smaller samples. They are usually less structured than questionnaires but this can improve the depth of information obtained. However, they are more difficult to analyse, and bias may creep in because people give answers that they think will please the interviewer.'

'Good point! What about focus groups?' Richard asked.

'I could access more people than I could with interviews but fewer than if I used questionnaires. The actual meetings could be highly structured, semi-structured or unstructured.'

'Any key advantages?' Richard asked.

'I think that the great strength is that people can bounce ideas off each other.'

'So focus groups can add another dimension in that sense.'

'Yes, I see what you mean. People don't discuss issues in questionnaires or interviews,' I said.

'Observations can also be a powerful data collection tool. They can be structured or unstructured and potentially the sample can be quite large. However, bias could be an issue if the researcher knows the group that is being observed, and just the presence of an observer can change how people act. But they do reveal what people do, which is a great strength.'

'So the data is authentic if it has been collected in a natural situation.'

'That all depends on the impact the observer has on the situation.'

'Observations must be good for triangulation as you get that "extra dimension" you mentioned earlier?' I said.

'Good point.'

'One thing, though. Are case studies and surveys mutually exclusive? Could I have a survey as part of my case study?'

'You need to assess the opinions of the participants somehow, so yes you could. Remember that these are not entirely separate strategies, so give me a link between case studies and action research.'

'I suppose that it's possible to do a case study on a piece of action research after it's happened. The instance could be the teacher, the pupils, the topic or the intervention.'

'Excellent, so these strategies aren't mutually exclusive and they can be combined in accordance with the demands of the research questions. So, a survey could be used to gather baseline evidence for action research.'

Sam's reflection

18 November

I do feel more comfortable with surveys. But I need to step outside my comfort zone. Essentially what I'm looking at is a range of strategies that can be combined in different ways and the label is then applied to the final combination. The strategies certainly seem to overlap.

I really need to focus my research on the professional practice of my colleagues and from that identify the most appropriate strategy. Maybe even then it wouldn't be absolutely 'right' and I would only know that after the event. I suppose that's what learning to be a researcher is all about, though I feel that it would take a lifetime to become an expert. Just look at Richard – he's had long enough, yet he still has his doubts.

Review of tutorial

Working at Master's level: Ethnographies

'You said you'd come back and look at other possible strategies.'

'So I did. Again Crotty (1998) and Denscombe (2010) are very strong in this area, so follow up what I say by dipping into them if you decide to use one of the following strategies.'

'OK.'

'Ethnographic studies are more commonly associated with Master's and PhD-level work. The word 'ethnography' comes from the Greek *ethnos*, meaning people, and *graphein*, meaning to write. So what sort of research does it relate to?'

'A strategy involving writing about people,' I suggested.

'Essentially yes, though in a broader context "people" refers to specific groups of people, their beliefs and behaviours. The groups could be defined or bounded by some common criterion such as religion or culture. The aim of your field work would be to gather enough data to present a highly detailed picture of the group being studied. You'd be interested in how the group viewed the world, the meanings that they gave to events and customs, rituals and beliefs. To get this level of detail you would have to immerse yourself in the lived lives of these people.'

'So I'd end up with a vast amount of data. Far more than I would need for my little research project.'

'Yes. Ethnographies are fascinating to read but they are very time-consuming because, to get the information you need, you have to win the trust of the people you are researching. But don't run away with the idea that ethnographic studies have to be done with some lost tribe in the Amazon. Great studies have been done on football hooligans, motor cycle gangs, and, perhaps most famously in British education, Willis's study of a group of school leavers in *Learning to Labour* (1981). They share many of the same characteristics as case studies but you really do collect mountains of detailed data. So I'd strongly advise against attempting an ethnography when you only have 5000 words to play with.'

'So, what other strategies might I think about at Master's level?'

Working at Master's level: Phenomenological studies

'You may also have heard of **phenomenology**.'

'That sounds like it's about studying phenomena such as events.'

'In a sense it is. But really it looks at how people interpret and react to the events and experiences (the phenomena) they encounter as they travel through life. Again look at both Crotty (1998) and Denscombe (2010) if you are interested in this approach. Basically it's concerned with how people interpret, understand and react to specific situations. As the researcher you explore people's experiences, understanding and reaction to particular events and how these help the person to build up their own view of reality. In truth, phenomenology is as much a branch of philosophy as it is research. Many of its followers think that the whole of human knowledge can be explained in this way.'

'It sounds interesting. But I don't think it's particularly relevant for my project.'

Working at Master's level: Grounded theory studies

'That's probably true, but **grounded theory** is well worth a mention. This strategy is interesting as it is almost the reverse of the traditional "scientific" approach to research in that data are first collected and categories identified. After a process of constant refinement and integration the resulting categories are then used to formulate theory. Traditionally, a literature review isn't carried out beforehand as it may influence the coding process and therefore the theory.'

'That does sound interesting.'

'It is, but beware. Glaser and Strauss (1967)'s original model suggests that you should go through a ten-stage process. Here's an outline of the process (➡*Handout 5.1*). The process is very stringent and time-consuming and suggests that you have to continue collecting data until such time as no new issues arise. At that point you have achieved saturation point and can start to build your theory.'

'That sounds like an open-ended commitment. I mean you wouldn't be able to predict how many interviews, observations or whatever you had to carry out in advance.'

'It's been revised since by Strauss and Corbin (1990) but it still has a number of protocols that you have to follow. Despite the potential problems, I think both undergraduates and postgraduate students should consider using the central idea of grounded theory in any piece of qualitative research.'

'What's the central idea?'

'That you try to collect data without imposing on it your own theory. Instead, collect and analyse the data and as far as is possible let the data speak for itself. Let the theory be suggested by the data rather than your own preconceived ideas and opinions.'

'But it sounds very time-consuming.'

'Which is why if you go down this route you describe your approach as inspired by the grounded theory approach rather than as a piece of grounded theory research. It's an approach you might use for an MA dissertation and, if you want to read around these ideas, have a look at what Keith Taber (2009) or Bryant and Charmaz (2010) have to say on the subject.'

Working at Master's level: Experiments and quasi-experiments

'OK, we're onto experiments and quasi-experiments.'

'They sound a bit too scientific for what I'm doing.'

'Well, they certainly originated in the positive/scientific paradigms. But they can be used in social research as well. Have a look at Newby (2010) and Cohen, Mannion and Morrison (2011) if you want to go deeper into this area, but for now let me outline the difference between experiments and quasi-experiments. In a scientific experiment the researcher tries to identify all the variables that are at play in a process and then either removes a variable, adds a variable or changes a variable and records the results that occur. For example, a typical experiment for a drugs trial would involve identifying a group of patients who had the same disease and were at a similar stage of the disease. Half of the patients would be given the new drug and the remaining half, the control group, would be given a placebo. Doctors would then monitor the progress of the disease in both groups and from that information decide how effective the drug was.'

'But in education it wouldn't be possible to have a control group,' I said.

Richard leaned forward, looking interested, 'Go on,' he said. 'Explain what you mean.'

'Well, groups of people don't share the same characteristics. Every class is different. So you couldn't have a control group, because the groups wouldn't "match up". Nor could you use two different teaching methods on the same group and assess which is best.'

'Why not'

'Because you'd have to teach the same topic to the group using each method. Obviously, once you'd covered the topic using method A, the group's understanding of and level of interest in the subject would change and this would be reflected in how they reacted to method B. So, any comparison would be undermined straightaway.'

'Very good. But you could try a quasi-experiment. For example, you could teach, say, *Romeo and Juliet* to a class using one teaching method and adopt another when you look at Miller's *Death of a Salesman* and then evaluate the results of both methods. It's not a scientific experiment, but it would still give you a good insight into which was the most effective teaching method with that group of learners.'

'I think teachers do quasi-experiments all the time – but they call it trial and error,' I said.

'That's probably true, but let me make one thing clear. You can use any of these approaches at Level 6 or 7 but, because of word limits, ethnographies and grounded theory approaches are perhaps more suited to Level 7 research. And because of the difficulties associated with set-up, validity and reliability, experiments require careful thought before you use them.'

'Fair enough. But what do I have to do differently at Level 7 if I use a survey, action research or a case study.'

'Have a look at what we said in Tutorial 1 about robustness. In addition to that you need to justify your choice of strategy more fully. It's no use having a theoretical discussion about the strengths and weaknesses of the strategy you have adopted and comparing it in purely academic terms with other strategies. You have to relate it to your actual research project and explain why it is the best strategy to use. You need to do this at Level 6 but it becomes vital at Level 7.'

'You mean demonstrate its "fitness for purpose"?'

'Exactly. Now why didn't I say that?'

Sam's reflection

20 November

OK, let's see. Ethnographies – too much detail required for my little research project of 5000 words. I'd spend so much time describing what I'd found that I'd have no space for analysis.

I like the sound of grounded theory. Especially as you don't require a literature review. Well, at least not until you've collected your data. But I don't like the idea of having to keep collecting data until no new issues are identified. I could still be finding new issues months after the assignment deadline. Of course, I could do as Richard suggested and just claim that my approach was "inspired by grounded theory". But I'm not trying to develop a theory. Just identify what teachers think are the most effective teaching methods to use with year 10 learners.

*I suppose an experiment would be quite useful, but I don't have the access or time to do experiments with students. Besides my participants are teachers not learners. And I'm pretty sure that the school would object to a trainee experimenting with a group of experienced teachers. I can just see the tabloid headlines: **Crazy trainee teacher tells peers that they've got it wrong.***

And as for action research what I'm doing doesn't involve changing anything. I'm not planning any interventions. So, it's not action research. It could be a case study. After all I have an 'instance' – teaching methods, and I'm using questionnaires and interviews. So maybe it's a case study. But will it produce a detailed picture of teaching methods? I don't think so.

Probably it's a survey. After all, most of my data will come from the questionnaires that I issue and this will be supported by a couple of interviews. Yeah, I think it's a survey. Of course, I could change my mind overnight. Why are there so many options and decisions in research?

Record of tutorial

Student: Sam Sylon   **Date: 7/11/XX**

SUMMARY OF KEY LEARNING POINTS

- The research process can be envisaged as a four-tier hierarchical process. Level 1 deals with the researcher's philosophical stance; Level 2, the research methodology, identifies the approach adopted by the researcher; Level 3, the research strategy, is about how the work will be structured – what vehicle will be used to undertake the work; and Level 4 deals with the data collection tools.

- Case studies use multiple data collection methods to get a three-dimensional picture of the instance under review.

- It is essential to define both the nature of the instance and the boundaries of the case study.

- The instance may be one person or a group of people, an organisation or an event.

- Criteria used to choose the instance include personal interest that it's typical or atypical, unique, extreme or convenient.

- Results from case studies are relatable but not generalisable.

- Evaluation criteria with other case studies could include similar time, place, people or organisation.

- Advantages of case studies include the use of multiple data collection methods and the ability to set boundaries and therefore the scale.

- Disadvantages include a lack of generalisability, possible bias and the influence of the researcher.

- Action research is fundamentally self-reflective and collaborative, and often focused on continuous professional development.

- Action research involves collecting baseline evidence, implementing an intervention, monitoring the effect of the intervention and finally producing an evaluation of the impact achieved by the intervention.

- Understanding of the approach varies and different models are prevalent. The key is to justify the approach in the context of your professional setting. ➡

- Reflective diaries are often crucial to providing evidence of continuing development and evaluation. They should not be purely descriptive and they should include diverse sources of evidence.

- Advantages of action research include relevance to practice, diverse evidence and authenticity.

- Disadvantages include a tendency toward formulaic approaches, possible controversy and a lack of analytical rigour.

- Surveys involve canvassing the attitudes, opinions or demographics of a population usually using questionnaires, interviews, focus groups or observations.

- Surveys very often involve sampling only part of the population.

- Email surveys are growing in popularity.

- Questionnaires, interviews, focus groups and observations all have advantages and disadvantages in such areas as sample size, structured/unstructured, authenticity and bias.

- If you are working at Master's level you should be considering if one of the following strategies may be appropriate:

  - Ethnographic approaches produce highly detailed description of people's culture, beliefs and rituals (eating everyday at McDonald's can be just as much a ritual as attending a religious ceremony). Because of the amount of data collected they are more suited to dissertations than shorter assignments.

  - Phenomenology is concerned with understanding people's interaction with and responses to a range of phenomena. Every interaction adds to the individual's understanding and interpretation of social reality. As with ethnographies, detail and depth is vital and for this reason phenomenological approaches are best suited to dissertations and theses.

  - Grounded theory involves collecting and coding data, and then building a theory from the data collected. The problem for students is that Glaser and Strauss's protocol requires the researcher to continue collecting data until saturation point has been reached and no new data is uncovered. This open-ended commitment makes it impractical for a student on a strict timetable. However, you may wish to use an approach to theory building that was inspired by Glaser and Strauss's work.

Remember it is not sufficient to just compare and contrast your research approach with other approaches in a purely academic discussion. You must demonstrate that your approach is 'fit for purpose' – that out of all the approaches you could have used your approach will produce the best outcomes for your research.

Agreed action points

Sam will:

- Review the research focus and questions and identify the most appropriate research strategy to adopt.
- Write a justification for the chosen strategy and compare this with the others, emphasising strengths and weaknesses in relation to the research focus.
- Evaluate the chosen strategy in terms of validity, reliability, ethics and bias.

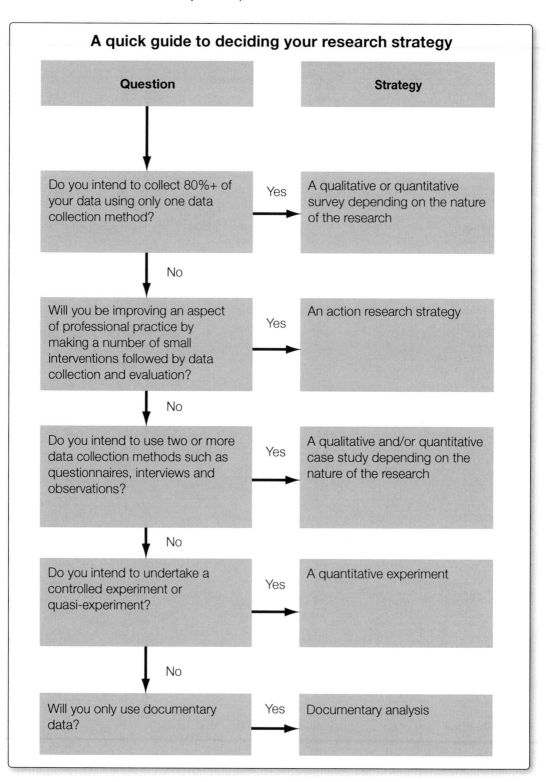

A quick guide to deciding your research strategy

Question		Strategy
Do you intend to collect 80%+ of your data using only one data collection method?	Yes →	A qualitative or quantitative survey depending on the nature of the research
↓ No		
Will you be improving an aspect of professional practice by making a number of small interventions followed by data collection and evaluation?	Yes →	An action research strategy
↓ No		
Do you intend to use two or more data collection methods such as questionnaires, interviews and observations?	Yes →	A qualitative and/or quantitative case study depending on the nature of the research
↓ No		
Do you intend to undertake a controlled experiment or quasi-experiment?	Yes →	A quantitative experiment
↓ No		
Will you only use documentary data?	Yes →	Documentary analysis

Handout 5.1

GLASER AND STRAUSS 10-STAGE GROUNDED THEORY PROTOCOL

Process	Activity	Comment
1	Collect data	Any source of textual data can be used
2	Transcribe data	It is necessary to provide full transcriptions
3	Develop categories	Use open coding to produce categories
4	Saturate categories	Further examples are gathered as the transcripts are analysed until no new examples of a particular category are found
5	Abstract definitions	Formal definitions, which define dimensions and properties are generated for each category
6	Theoretical sampling	Choose theoretically relevant samples from the data to test and develop categories further
7	Axial coding	Explore and test the relationships between categories
8	Theoretical integration	A core category is identified and related to other subsidiary categories by means of a coding paradigm, and links with existing theories are developed
9	Grounding the theory	The emergent theory is grounded by returning to the data and validating it against actual segments of the text
10	Filling the gaps	Missing detail is filled in by collection of further data

Adapted from Bartlett and Payne (1997)

GATHERING YOUR DATA – INTERVIEWS AND OBSERVATIONS

Aim of tutorial

In conjunction with Tutorial 7, this tutorial will help you select and evaluate the most appropriate data collection tool/s for your research. Each method is described and evaluated.

Areas covered in this tutorial

Sam's reflection

22 November

At last! Today we'll be discussing something that I understand. No more research paradigms or research strategies. Instead, simple straightforward data collection methods. I think Richard is going to look at interviews, observations and questionnaires. I've used interviews and questionnaires in the past to collect data for assignments. I've also observed newly qualified teachers and peers and been observed by my mentor and Professional Development Tutor from the university. So, there shouldn't be too many surprises, but then again Richard has a habit of looking at things from odd angles so I'd better not get overconfident.

Review of tutorial

Richard was surfing the Web when I entered. He looked up and waved me into a seat and logged off before saying, 'Hi, how are you?'

'Fine. I'm looking forward to today's session because at last it's something I have some experience of.'

'That's great. It makes things easier if you have some practical experience of what we're discussing. What I want to look at over the next two sessions are four common methods of data collection – namely, interviews, observations, questionnaires and documentation. Today we'll look at interviews and observations. Not surprisingly all of the key books that I identified on the Recommended reading list deal with these collection methods and, as we work through the tutorial, I might make a couple of additional suggestions. So what methods have you used in the past?'

'I've used both interviews and questionnaires.'

Arranging an interview or observation and agreeing the ground rules

'Excellent. But before we get into discussing the data collection methods, I want to talk a little bit about how you approach the people whom you want to collect data from. The first thing you have to remember is that they're doing you a favour, so treat them with consideration and respect. If I want to interview or observe someone, I like to make personal contact with them and explain the purpose of my research before asking if they're willing to be involved. If they say "yes", I follow up my conversation with a detailed letter or email confirming the nature of the research and the conditions upon which they are taking part.'

'What would you include in your email?'

'I'd confirm the date, time and venue of the interview or observation. You should always try to see the person on their "turf" not yours and if that's not possible on neutral ground.'

'I've read about this,' I said. 'It's a matter of putting them at their ease and limiting any fears or nerves that they might have.'

'Exactly! I'd also confirm that their anonymity will be protected at all times. Secondly, I would make it clear that they have the right to withdraw from the research at any stage up to the point when the final report is published. And finally I would explain to them how they could access my completed research.'

'So, basically you pick up the main ethical issues and make sure that they understand the research and why they're taking part.'

'That's right.'

'Do you have an example of a letter that I could use?'

'There is one on my website **www.routledge.com/9780273774792**.'

Providing information to participants and dealing with anonymity and confidentiality

'Would you give them a copy of the interview or observation schedule in advance?'

'You have been reading up on this,' he said, with a smile. 'I like to provide my participants with a copy of any data collection instrument that I intend to use in advance. It gives them a chance to think about the type of issues that I'm interested in.'

'I asked because I'm not sure that it's a good idea. If you tell them what you're looking for it gives them a chance to prepare an answer or change their behaviour.'

'In theory that's true, but in reality people are too busy to prepare an answer in advance or to plan a change in their behaviour just for you. They might do that for an Ofsted ...'

'But I'm not worth it,' I said, smiling.

'I'm glad to see you understand your place in the scheme of things. What I was going to say was that the advantage of sending a copy of the questions or observation schedule in advance is that it demonstrates that you are not trying to catch them out.'

'What about confidentiality?'

'I'm always cautious about promising confidentiality because I intend to write about what the people say and do. So it is difficult to claim that I'll treat what they reveal in confidence. That's why I emphasise anonymity (➡ **Tutorials 2 and 4**). Of course, during the interview or after the interview has ended people often tell you something "in confidence". And you can't divulge that unless you have a legal obligation, such as child protection issues. I once had a respondent who at the end of the interview said, "Now I'll tell you what I really think about the Principal", but I couldn't use it because it was told to me in confidence.'

Sam's reflection

23 November

I hadn't given much thought to the actual mechanics of arranging the interviews or observations. Previously, I'd just done things informally, but Richard wants me to include a copy of any formal communication that I have with my respondents as an appendix. When you think about it, he's right. This module is all about learning how to do a small-scale piece of research, so I need to provide evidence of what I've done and how I've done it. And that includes the management and organisation of the project. In addition, if I'm ever involved in a large-scale research project I'll have to deal with these issues, so I might as well practise these skills now.

I agree with what Richard says about confidentiality. But I'm not so sure about sending the interview questions to the respondents in advance. I know several people who would think about their answers if they knew what the questions were going to be, and most teachers I know change their teaching approach when they know they're being observed.

Review of tutorial

Types of interview

'The first thing I want to stress is that the type of interviews and observations available to you can be plotted on a continuum that runs from highly structured to completely unstructured.'

'And in the middle you have semi-structured,' I suggested.

'Exactly. In a completely structured interview you'd have a long list of questions, such as, name, age, gender, job title, length of time in present post, educational experience, etc. and your questions would be very specific.'

'But that's more like a questionnaire than an interview,' I said.

'Yes. But it's an interview because you are sitting in front of the person asking the questions. It would be described as 'highly structured' because as the interviewer you've decided the parameters of the discussion in advance, and the type of question you're asking requires specific information from the respondent, which means that they can't digress from your agenda.'

'That sounds like one very boring interview.'

'It probably is, but it can be used with young children or any respondent who might have difficulty completing a questionnaire. At the other end of the continuum you have the completely unstructured interview where you sit down with someone and say something like "Tell me about your experience as a teacher". That's a very open question and it invites the respondent to tell you whatever they think is important about their experiences.'

I didn't like the sound of that. I had visions of growing old as someone told me their life story in stultifying detail. 'I'm not keen on that as a type of interview either.'

'Very few small-scale research projects use this approach because of the time it takes to carry out and analyse a series of unstructured interviews.'

'I think I prefer semi-structured interviews.'

Shared characteristics of interviews and observations

'Most people do. Semi-structured interviews sit in the middle of the continuum. But before we discuss interviews in a bit more detail, I'd like to emphasise that the same range of options applies to observations. You can have observations where you could go into a classroom with a highly detailed schedule of actions that you expect to observe and as you see each action you place a tick in the appropriate box. Or you could just go in with a blank sheet of paper and record anything that caught your attention. Interviews and observations share the same common underlying structure. Here, this handout should clarify what I am saying.' (➡*Handout 6.1*)

Sam's reflection

23 November

I don't like the idea of either highly structured or highly unstructured data collection instruments. Structured approaches only allow you to collect data on issues that you've identified in advance. Effectively, you'd be saying you already know what all the important issues are. They wouldn't reveal an issue that you hadn't already identified. I could easily miss important stuff if I used that approach. However, the unstructured approach involves collecting loads of data, much of which might be irrelevant. Not to mention that it would take me forever to analyse. No, I'll stick with my semi-structured approach.

Review of tutorial

When to use interviews

'So let's look at interviews in a bit more detail. When would you use interviews as a method of data collection?'

'When I need to find out people's views on an issue,' I said confidently.

'If that is all you want to do, why not use a questionnaire? After all it would be easier and you could send it to more people than you could reasonably interview?'

'True, but I'd use interviews when I wanted to explore people's attitudes or beliefs in depth. It would be hard to do that using a questionnaire.'

'That's true. Semi-structured and unstructured interviews do provide a depth of information that you can't get from a questionnaire,' Richard said.

'But structured interviews don't, and unstructured interviews would take too long.'

When to use semi-structured interviews

'Which is why most single researchers use semi-structured interviews. The researcher knows the broad areas on which they wish to collect information and they ask a series of open-ended questions that cover just those areas. The use of open-ended questions allows the respondent to express their own views on the issue. If they start to digress too much, the researcher can pull them back by asking a supplementary question or saying something like "That's an interesting observation on the Governors' Christmas party but could you tell me a little more about the teaching methods you use?" '

'So you've heard about our Governors' Christmas party?' I said, laughing. 'But if semi-structured interviews are so useful, what's the point of structured and unstructured interviews?'

When to use structured and unstructured interviews

'As I said, the structured interview can be used instead of a questionnaire when you're dealing with children or people who either can't read or can't understand a questionnaire or with any group that is likely to give a poor response rate. In a way what you're doing is delivering a questionnaire personally. The unstructured interview is really useful when you're investigating a new topic and want to find out about the major themes and ideas contained within it. They're particularly valuable when you're undertaking an in-depth study of people's experiences over an extended period of time – for example, their experiences at school. However, they take up a lot of time, as issues are explored in depth and data analysis can be a nightmare.'

'So the type of interview that you conduct is determined by what you want to find out and the people that you intend to interview.'

'Correct. But you also have to take into account the time that you have available and the word limit on your assignment. You have to be practical. Think of Goldilocks. The structured interviews are too small, like Baby Bear's bed: they may not produce enough data for many small-scale projects. The unstructured interview is the equivalent of Daddy Bear's bed: they may take too much time and produce too much data. But the semi-structured interview is just right, like Mummy Bear's bed. There's a nice little series of books published by the University of Glasgow. The one on semi-structured interviews is by Erici Dever (2003) which you should check out.'

Sam's reflection

24 November

I can't believe that my lecturer has just used Goldilocks and the Three Bears to explain a concept in research theory. I bet if I told the tabloid papers, there would be an outcry about the dumbing-down of education standards.

But the truth is, I think it's a good example which I need to apply to all aspects of my research. The number of words I have available limits the amount of literature I can include, the number of data collection tools I can use and the number of people I can collect data from. I need to be selective in choosing my sources too. Similarly, with the amount of data I collected – there is only so much I can report and analyse in my findings. It's quality not quantity that I need to go for. I must be selective.

Drafting my interview questions

'How would you suggest that I go about deciding on my interview questions?' I asked. 'I've always found this difficult.'

'This is really important. We often see interview questions that have little or no relevance to the student's research questions. This means that, however interesting the data is that you collect, it won't help you answer your research questions. Start by looking at your research questions. Take each one in turn and try to break it down into various themes. This will give you a list of words or phrases that you can use to formulate your initial interview questions. Write these questions out. When you've finished, look at your list of possible interview questions and eliminate any duplicates. Then look and see if any questions can be amalgamated. Only after you have done this do you want to start editing the questions.'

'You mean check your questions as you do with a questionnaire?'

'Precisely. Check that your questions are unambiguous and that you've not asked any leading questions.'

'You mean like, "Would you agree with me that . . ." '

'Exactly. You want the interviewees' views and therefore you must do everything you can to avoid influencing their answers. This includes thinking carefully about the order in which you ask the questions.'

'Why would the order be important?'

'Sometimes the order of the questions can lead the interviewee in a particular direction. For example once Dorothy was on the "yellow brick road" she was led inexorably to Oz. You can do the same thing with your participants if you aren't careful.'

I knew that Richard wouldn't be able to provide an exact answer to my next question but I asked it anyway. 'In a 25/30-minute, semi-structured interview how many questions should I ask?'

'That's like asking "how long is a piece of string?" I would suggest that five or six is the maximum. After all, they have to be broad enough to encourage the person to express their views in some detail.'

'And the first question should be used to put them at their ease?'

'Yes, but don't ask a question that has little bearing on your research. That's just a waste of your time. So ask an easy question that is relevant.'

'OK, but how many interviews do I need to do?'

'We're back to that piece of string again. In reality you conduct as many interviews as are necessary to answer your research questions. But usually for a 5000-word assignment I would say four should be sufficient.'

'Of course!' I said, remembering one of the early tutorials.' (➡ *Tutorial 1*) 'You said that an average 30-minute interview produced four or five sheets of A4 single-spaced transcript. So, four interviews would produce 16 pages or 8000 words and the findings section of my 5000-word assignment will only be about 2000 words.'

'So, maybe you could get away with three half-hour interviews or four 20/25-minute interviews. But your decision must be based on collecting enough useful data to answer your research questions. It is a matter of judgement.'

Sam's reflection

24 November

First 'Goldilocks', now the 'Wizard of Oz', what next, Cinderella? Still it was good advice to analyse my research questions as the first stage in writing my interview questions. That way I can make sure that the questions I ask relate directly to my research questions. I suppose drawing up an interview schedule is a bit like dancing. We can all move about on the dance floor but the trained dancer really does stand out as does a good interview schedule.

What Richard said about the number of questions seems sensible. Basically he's allowing five minutes for the person to answer a question.

There's something nagging at the back of my mind about research questions and their link to interview questions. What is it?

Got it! Once I've written my interview questions I need to check that they're capable of producing the data I need to answer each of my research questions and that I haven't missed anything in the editing. I can do this by drawing up a list of my research questions and a list of the interview questions side by side and linking them together with lines showing which interview question helps answer which research question, maybe like this:

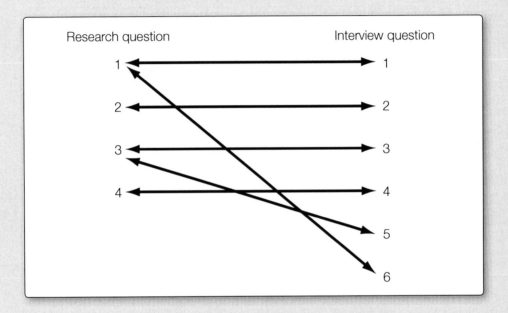

What I must avoid is the situation where I ask an interview question that has no links with my research questions. If I do that I'm just wasting time. But what is even more important is that I don't end up with a research question that has no links to any of my interview questions. If that happens, it means that I wouldn't have any data to answer that question! I think my diagram is really useful. I wonder if Richard uses something similar.

Review of tutorial

Recording interviews

'Do I need to tape and transcribe every interview that I undertake?' I asked.

'That is a difficult question to answer. I think best practice would suggest that you tape and transcribe every interview. However, there are problems with such an approach. For example, not everyone likes to be recorded and, if your subject refuses to be taped, you have to respect their decision. But if your respondent is happy to be taped you still need to decide if you're going to transcribe the whole tape or just those sections that you're particularly interested in. If you cherry-pick "the best sections" to transcribe, you run the risk of ignoring data which appears boring but is actually important. A full transcription of a 30-minute interview takes time – maybe two or three hours – so you have to weigh the advantages and disadvantages of your approach.'

'But some people just take notes when interviewing. Is that poor practice?'

'It depends. Each researcher has to justify the approach they take. So, if the researcher believed that the use of a recorder would distract the respondent and cause them to censor their answers, she might decide to take notes in the meeting or to write up her notes of the meeting immediately after the interview.'

'I would have thought that it would be better to take notes in the meeting.'

'Possibly, but while you are taking notes you are not concentrating on what the person is saying. This can distract the interviewee and you may fail to pick up on body language or something important.'

'This interviewing business isn't easy,' I said.

'No it isn't. Interviewing is a skill and like any other skill it has to be learnt, and the only way you can improve is through practice. Remember you want to find out what the respondent thinks or feels about an issue, so you need to let them do the talking and through your body language make it clear that you are actively listening to them. Most people like to be asked for their opinion and will welcome the opportunity to expound their views. However, don't get into a discussion with them and tell them what you think even if they ask for your views. Side-step such requests by saying "we can talk about my views later". Just ask your questions and give the interviewee the time and space to respond. Don't be impatient with them and jump in to fill silences and never argue or appear shocked by anything they say. Instead, encourage them to expand on issues of interest by saying something like "that's very interesting; could you tell me a little bit more about it?"

'You said previously that I need to include copies of each transcript as an appendix when I submit my work . . .'

'Increasingly colleges and universities require you to do this. But some just want to see a blank copy of the interview schedule.'

I sighed under my breath. Another load of paper to attach to the report.

Sam's reflection

25 November

I think I'll record and transcribe each interview. It will take a bit of time but once I have the full transcripts in front of me I'll be able to compare and contrast what each interviewee said on every question. I'll also be able to do searches using F5 in Word to find specific words and phrases across each script. Of course, if my interviewees don't want to be recorded, I'll have to take very short notes in the interview and write them up as soon as we've finished. I hope no one objects to being recorded!

Review of tutorial

Participant and non-participant observations

'So, if you use interviews to find out what people say they do, why do we need observations?' asked Richard.

'Because people don't always do what they say they do,' I ventured.

'Precisely! Very often people are unaware that there's a difference between what they say they do and what they actually do. For example, it is not unusual for teachers to describe their teaching style as "learner-centred". But when you observe them teach, they might use teacher-centred methods most of the time. Therefore, to find out what's actually happening you need to do some observations.'

'Are you saying teachers are self-delusional?' I asked with malicious glee.

'No', he smiled. 'I'm saying everyone is delusional. None of us ever really knows how we and our actions are perceived by other people.'

'That sounds like my Head. But surely it's hard to get people to act naturally if they know they're being observed?'

'That's true, but there are two types of observation: **participant** and **non-participant**. An Ofsted inspector who sits at the back of the class watching you teach is using non-participative observation. They're alien to the classroom and don't take part in the lesson. Their presence changes the behaviour of both the teacher and the children.'

'It would certainly change mine!' I said.

Richard laughed and then continued. 'Participant observation occurs when the researcher collects data at the same time as they engage in their normal activities. For example, a teacher might be teaching a class, but she may also be observing how learners react to certain teaching methods. She doesn't record her findings in the class but waits until the end of the lesson and then writes her notes up.'

'What you're saying is that she carries out her observations in secret without telling anyone, and that way people act normally.'

'Not really. Remember that one of the cardinal ethical requirements is that you obtain informed consent. (➡ *Tutorial 4*) So, if you want to conduct participant observation on a group of learners or teachers, you have to ask their permission.'

'But wouldn't that defeat the whole purpose of participant observation. The respondent would know that you are looking at them and act differently,' I argued.

'Well, the way I get round that is to explain the purpose of my research and ask the participants if I can observe them as part of my project. If they agree, I leave it for a week or two before I do the observation. By then they've forgotten about my research and have reverted to acting normally.'

'That's a bit sneaky isn't it?'

'Not really.' He said this with a smile that suggested butter wouldn't melt in his mouth. 'I've obtained their informed consent and explained what I intend to do, so I'm not deceiving them.'

Sam's reflection

25 November

I quite like the idea of participant observation. It allows me to act out my spy fantasies and observe people without them knowing. It's probably the best way of capturing what people actually do. They don't realise or have forgotten that they're being watched and so they act more naturally than they would in an interview or a non-participant observation. I could make a note of what they say, too. I would imagine that, if it's done properly, you could collect some really good data from participant observations. Mind you, you'd probably have to do a number of observations over a period of time to gather sufficient data.

Review of tutorial

Recording observational data

'From what you say it sounds as if non-participant observers are likely to use observation checklists prepared in advance.'

'I think that's probably true. The non-participant observer is more likely to use a checklist to record what they see. For example, they might have a category "child asks teacher a question". Every time this occurs they would place a tick against that activity. At the end of the session they would add up the number of ticks and be able to report that on 13 occasions a child asked the teacher a question.'

'Does this mean that a researcher using participant observation is likely to use unstructured observations?'

'Participant observers are unlikely to use a written schedule but that doesn't mean that they haven't got a list of items to look out for in their mind. The participant observer will have considered what actions or activities are relevant to their research in advance and will look for these. During the observation they may make the odd rough note to remind them of what they've observed or heard, but it is more likely that they'll find a few minutes after the observation to jot down some notes. Unlike the structured observation they wouldn't be able to specify the number of times a learner asked a question of the teacher but they would be able to say something like, "the children regularly asked the teacher questions".'

'So they would write up what they saw as a series of notes and use that as the record of data collected?'

'Or they could write up their observations in the form of a reflective journal. This is a really useful approach because it allows the researcher to reflect upon and become engaged with the events observed. They can then interpret them at their leisure.'

'Do you have any examples of interview or observation schedules that I could look at?'

'Yes, of course. You will find them on my website **www.routledge.com/ 9780273774792.**   But you should also check out Simpson and Tuson's (2003) book on observations.'

Sam's reflection

25 November

From what Richard has said I think that I could use semi-structured observations to check out if the teachers actually use the teaching methods that they say they do. What I now have to decide is: do I use participant or non-participant observation? I think I'll get a more accurate picture of what is going on if I use participant observation – but will I remember it all when I come to write up my notes. Maybe I could just jot down a word or two during the session to remind me of key events. Or maybe I could do a couple of participant observations and a couple of non-participant observations. I need to think about this.

Review of tutorial

Working at Master's level

'That's about it for today,' Richard said, 'except for some advice about working at Master's level. Everything I've said above applies to working at Master's level. But you need to go a bit further.'

'In what way?'

Aligning my research

'You have to make sure that the focus of your research is reflected in your research questions and that your research tools will give you the data you need to answer your research questions. Basically you have to ensure alignment between research aims, questions and data collection tools.'

'And how do I ensure that?'

'Here's a handout which shows you what I mean. (➡**Handout 6.2**) The area covered by Box 1 represents your focal paragraph or topic that you are going to research. In Box 2 I've split that topic down into 3 research questions but the box remains the same size and the research questions only cover the topic you are looking at. I haven't gone off on a tangent and written a research question that doesn't relate to the focus of my research or which spills outside the area of the box. In Box 3 I've split the research questions into six interview questions, it could be eight questions …'

'But they still relate directly back to your research questions. And the fourth and fifth boxes, that deal with questionnaire and observations, do the same. What you're doing is showing in a diagrammatic form how you drill down into your research topic, while always checking that you are only collecting the data you need to answer your research question.'

'Correct. You will also have to provide a stronger justification for your choice of data collection methods. For example, why have you used individual interviews rather than a focus group or a questionnaire?'

Focus groups

'A focus group?'

'Yes. A focus group is where you get between five and eight people in a room and ask them to give their views on a series of questions. The questions will be very similar to those you would use in semi-structured interview but, because there are several people present, the group will end up discussing the question between themselves and different viewpoints will quickly emerge. If it's important that you collect a wide variety of views, you might want to think about using both interviews and focus groups. But there are problems with focus groups. Care to say what?'

I sat for a few seconds and then replied, 'If you record the session it could be difficult to know who is talking and if there is a particularly strong character in the group they may monopolise the meeting.'

'Good. But you could get around who is talking by videoing the session and as chair you can control the strong characters and make sure that the less extrovert members of the group have a fair say. But what might be a justification for using an interview rather than a focus group?'

Again I sat and thought before replying. 'People may say things in a one-to-one situation that they wouldn't say in a group,' I said doubtfully.

Justifying my choice of data collection methods

'Correct. It's no good just listing the strengths and weaknesses of each approach. You have to spell out the strengths and weaknesses as they apply to your particular research. If you are thinking of using focus groups, Sage have a good book in their Qualitative Research Kit series on Focus groups. I think the author is Barber (2008).

'So, as with my choice of research strategy, I have to show how my choice of methods is the best fit for my particular research.'

'Yes. Similarly you'd have to justify why you choose participant research over non-participant research ...'

'In terms of my specific research and not just a list of general strengths and weaknesses?'

'Yes. Well that's enough for today. See you next week.'

Record of tutorial

Student: Sam Sylon   **Date: 22/11/XX**

SUMMARY OF KEY LEARNING POINTS

- When arranging interviews and observations follow up any initial contact with participants with an email or letter.

- Confirm date, time and venue in writing.

- In order to address ethical issues, include statements in the letter/email concerning anonymity, the participant's right to withdraw at any time and details of how they can access the final report/results.

- Consider sending the participants a copy of the interview or observation schedule in advance.

- Both observations and interviews can be located on a spectrum that runs from highly structured to totally unstructured.

- Interviews are used to collect data on people's attitudes, beliefs, feelings and opinions.

- The type of interview used depends on how much you know about the subject and the abilities of respondents.

- It is vital to refer to the research questions when drawing up the interview questions and the observation schedule. Use a chart to confirm that the interview or observation schedule will collect the data required to answer the research questions.

- Consider how to record the interview – tape record or take notes. When deciding what approach to take, think about analysis of data collected.

- Observations reveal what people do, they do not explain why they acted in a particular manner.

- When using observations consider which method of observation is most suitable – participant or non-participant observation. The choice depends on what the researcher already knows, what they want to find out and the attitudes of the respondents.

- Consider how to record observations – use detailed schedules, notes written up during or after the observation or a reflective journal. ➡

- At Master's level it is essential that there is a direct link between your research focus, your research questions and the data you collect. Check that there is clear alignment between all three.

- Interviews are time-consuming to arrange, hold, transcribe and analyse. Focus groups enable you to collect the views of a wide range of people at one meeting but inevitably they do not provide the same depth of personal information.

- If you use focus groups you must ensure that all participants have the chance to air their views.

- As in other areas of Master's level work you must fully justify your choice of data collection methods. Your argument should demonstrate that your data collection methods are the most appropriate to use for your specific research project.

Agreed action points

Sam will:

- Decide if interviews and questionnaires or just questionnaires will be used in the research.

- Review the example letter to participants on my website **www.routledge.com/ 9780273774792** and draft a covering letter to accompany any questionnaire or interview schedule that may be used.

- Check that the intended data collection tool/s (interview schedule/observation schedule/questionnaire) is capable of collecting the data required to answer all research questions.

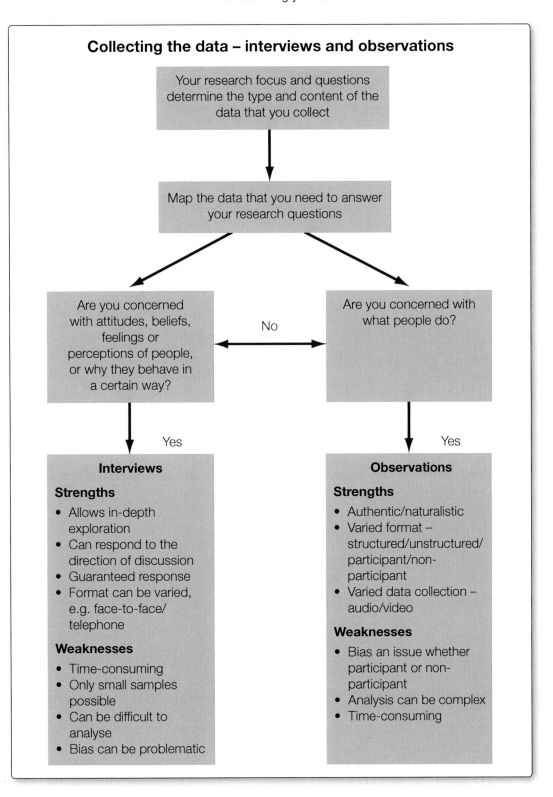

Collecting the data – interviews and observations

Your research focus and questions determine the type and content of the data that you collect

Map the data that you need to answer your research questions

Are you concerned with attitudes, beliefs, feelings or perceptions of people, or why they behave in a certain way?

No

Are you concerned with what people do?

Yes

Yes

Interviews

Strengths

- Allows in-depth exploration
- Can respond to the direction of discussion
- Guaranteed response
- Format can be varied, e.g. face-to-face/ telephone

Weaknesses

- Time-consuming
- Only small samples possible
- Can be difficult to analyse
- Bias can be problematic

Observations

Strengths

- Authentic/naturalistic
- Varied format – structured/unstructured/ participant/non-participant
- Varied data collection – audio/video

Weaknesses

- Bias an issue whether participant or non-participant
- Analysis can be complex
- Time-consuming

Handout 6.1

CONTINUUM OF INTERVIEWS AND OBSERVATIONS

Approach	Examples	Strengths	Weaknesses
Highly structured: The researcher determines in advance what information they wish to collect.	Questions/ categories are pre-specified in detail and allow for only specific answers, e.g. yes, no, age, agree, disagree, behaviour seen/not seen, count.	Data analysis is simplified.	The researcher's view of what is important dominates data collected and restrains respondent from expressing their views.
Semi-structured: The researcher knows the broad headings that they wish to collect data on but is open to the unexpected provided it is broadly relevant to their research.	Questions/ categories are broader. Questions and observation prompts are seen as starting point for the collection of data rather than the end.	Reduced researcher bias. The respondents' actions or words are used to determine what is important. This increases the likelihood that data new to the researcher will be uncovered.	Increased variability in the issues covered leading to increased problems of comparability and data analysis.
Unstructured: The researcher has an interest in a particular issue but does not wish to limit the research to parameters that they impose either arbitrarily or because of their lack of knowledge.	Questions are broad and open ended. Observation schedules may be 'blank' or composed of just a few prompts.	Researcher bias is minimised and the range of issues identified expanded very significantly.	Comparability between data sets is significantly decreased making analysis much more difficult and time-consuming.

Handout 6.2

STAYING WITHIN THE BOUNDARIES SET BY YOUR RESEARCH FOCUS

The following graphic shows how the area covered by your research focus remains constant. Each data collection tool simply asks questions or looks for events that are covered by the research focus. As a researcher you need to collect data that is within the boundaries set by your research focus. If you go beyond these boundaries, the data collected will not be relevant to your focus or help you answer your research questions. *Note* the number of questions or factors specified in a particular box is for illustrative purposes only. The number required will vary from one piece of research to the next.

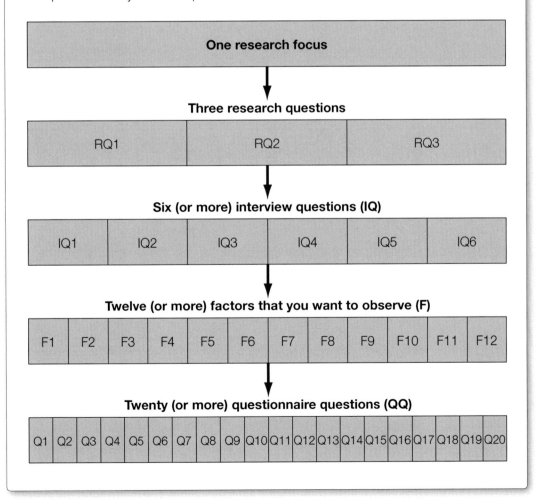

One research focus

Three research questions

| RQ1 | RQ2 | RQ3 |

Six (or more) interview questions (IQ)

| IQ1 | IQ2 | IQ3 | IQ4 | IQ5 | IQ6 |

Twelve (or more) factors that you want to observe (F)

| F1 | F2 | F3 | F4 | F5 | F6 | F7 | F8 | F9 | F10 | F11 | F12 |

Twenty (or more) questionnaire questions (QQ)

| Q1 | Q2 | Q3 | Q4 | Q5 | Q6 | Q7 | Q8 | Q9 | Q10 | Q11 | Q12 | Q13 | Q14 | Q15 | Q16 | Q17 | Q18 | Q19 | Q20 |

GATHERING YOUR DATA – DOCUMENTS AND QUESTIONNAIRES

Aim of tutorial

In conjunction with Tutorial 6, this tutorial will help you select and evaluate the most appropriate data collection tool/s for your research. Each method is described and evaluated.

Areas covered in this tutorial

29 November

I've had a busy week trying to review last week's tutorial tape, write up my notes and prepare for today's session. Still the course is almost over. Now's not the time to slow down. We're looking at questionnaires and documentation today. It should be really useful as I am fairly sure that I'll use questionnaires as my main data collection tool. I think I'll issue them to all the teachers who teach year 9–10 in my school. That will give me much more coverage than I could ever achieve if I were to interview them all. What I'm not so sure about is what does Richard mean by documentation? When we last talked about documentation it was with reference to the literature review. Unless he's on about statistics such as exam and SATs results.

Review of tutorial

Richard was reading a book when I entered. He appeared to be scribbling notes in the margin.

'I hope that's not a library book,' I said, trying to tease him.

'No. It's a book which I have been asked to review. I find that I understand things better if I engage with a book and have a conversation with the author about their ideas rather than just passively absorb what they have to say. You should try it.'

'So you must be one of those people who like second-hand books that people have written notes in?'

Documents as a source of data

'Only if the writing is neat! But enough of this idle chit-chat, you're here to work,' he said in his best imitation of Scrooge. 'Today I want to look at questionnaires and documentation as sources of data. We've already looked at the use of diverse sources for your literature review, but some sources can also provide data for your findings. What type of documents do you think you could use for data in a research report?'

'I've been thinking about this. Previously you said that I could include documents and reports from the Government, the TDA, Ofsted, the local education authority and my school in the literature review. So, I assume that the type of documentary data that goes in the findings would be restricted to statistics on achievement and suchlike.'

'That's interesting. I did say that official reports and documentation could be used in the literature review. Very often such documents are used to contextualise the issues that you're looking at and to locate your work in the broader picture. But the content of official documents can also be used as data and not just the statistics contained in them. For example, if the focus of your research was the impact of school inspections on teachers, you might well include data and comments from Ofsted reports on a range of schools. In reality what determines if a particular document is used as a source of literature or data is the focus of your research. Do you understand?'

'I think so,' I said doubtfully.

'Let me give you an example from your own research. You could use Ofsted reports on teaching methods in your literature review to contextualise the issues you want to explore. But you could also use the Ofsted report on your school's teaching methods as data.'

'So, what you're saying is that documents which contain data directly relevant to my research questions can be used as data just like data from an interview. But if it's discussing the subject of my research in just general terms, then it's literature?'

Using official statistics

'Correct. However, you're right when you say that official documents are often used as a source of statistical data. For example, if you wanted to compare your school's performance against the local, regional or national averages on a whole range of measures, then a chat with your Head, local education advisor or a search of Google Scholar will more than likely reveal a whole raft of statistical reports and returns that you could use. The UK Statistics Authority and the Organisation for Economic Co-operation and Development (OECD) are all useful sources.'

Be critical of data in official documents

'But you said that I should be critical of everything I read. So how much reliance can I put on data in any official report and the data in it?'

'That's a really good point. What I think I said was that you need to critically evaluate every source that you use. Disraeli once said that "there are lies, damn lies and statistics". So you need to know at least two things about any set of statistics before you rely on them. Firstly, how were they calculated and secondly, for what purpose were they calculated. To give you an idea of how statistics can be warped to support any argument, I remember a newspaper headline not so long ago which read "Fifty per cent of all schools are below average". What makes you think that the writer was a critic of the Government's education policy?'

'But that sort of bias could also apply to reports that contained few or no statistics.'

'Absolutely! As I say, the golden rule in research is to critically evaluate every document and piece of information you rely on for data or literature and think about the motives that the authors might have for taking a particular view. Go back and have a look at what I said previously (➡ *Tutorial 2*) and look again at Hart (1998) to remind yourself of key issues. And while you're at it, Bryman (2008) has an interesting chapter on using documents as data in his huge book on social science research.'

I grimaced at the mention of the word 'huge', and Richard said, 'It's only a chapter. It won't kill you.'

'Easy for you to say.'

Richard ignored my pretence at rebellion and continued as if he hadn't been interrupted. 'And don't forget to consider the provenance of whatever it is that you are reading. Of course, there are practical limits to how far you can take this approach. It would be impossible to carry out a minute and detailed scrutiny of every document that you use. What you want to do is cultivate a critical and enquiring mindset. Using the available evidence, you need to ask yourself whether the claims made in the document are reasonable.

Sam's reflection

30 November

I'm still not entirely certain that I understand the difference between documents that I use as data and documents that I include in my literature review. Let's think how I can distinguish the two. This requires a cup of tea and a fig roll.

I suppose the easiest way to decide is to ask, 'does this document contain data that directly helps me to answer one or more of my research questions?' If it does, then it is data. If it only contains data that contextualises the issues I'm looking at, or which I use to explore and challenge the data I've collected, then it's literature. That's not bad as a rough guide.

Review of tutorial

Questionnaires

'Right, let's talk about questionnaires. Last time I said that interviews and observations could be located on a continuum from highly structured to completely unstructured. (➡ *Tutorial 6*) Well, questionnaires can also fit onto that continuum. You could have a highly structured questionnaire that only asked closed questions such as age, gender, et cetera, or you could have one that asked people to write about their views on a particular subject.'

'I don't think that you'd get many responses from a totally unstructured questionnaire. It would take too long to complete,' I said.

'And that's why you very seldom see an unstructured questionnaire. Research seems to indicate that, if a questionnaire can't be completed in six to eight minutes, most people throw it in the bin. Of course, if you give your respondents some inducement, such as entry into a prize draw or free shopping vouchers, people may be willing to spend longer on the task.'

'But, surely, if I give the questionnaire to colleagues they would be willing to spend longer completing it?'

'You'd think so, but I wouldn't bet on it. They get bored and you don't want to annoy them with long-winded and poorly designed questionnaires. Remember . . .'

'I know,' I interrupted. 'They're doing me a favour, so I need to keep my questionnaire short and snappy.'

'Correct. But that doesn't mean that you can only ask closed questions. A well-designed questionnaire can contain a mixture of open and closed questions. So you tell me what sort of questions might appear on a questionnaire?'

Types of questions found in questionnaires

'You can have closed questions such as name, gender, date of birth or multiple-choice questions where you just tick the correct one. Then there are those where you are asked to ring those words that apply to you, and of course there are the Likert-scale questions where you say if you agree strongly, agree, neither agree nor disagree, disagree and disagree strongly . . .'

'That's pretty good. You could also ask people to rank things in order of preference. For example, please rank the following teaching methods in order of personal preference where 1 is your favourite and 7 your least liked. This handout (➡*Handout 7.1*) lists the most common type of questions used and gives you an example of each. There are further examples on my website **www.routledge.com/9780273774792** and you should also have a look at Munn and Drever's (2007) short book on questionnaires. What you need to do is decide what information you need to collect and select the right type of question to elicit that information. What this means in practice is that most good questionnaires contain a variety of question types. So, how do you check that your questionnaire is going to collect the information that you need?'

Now was the time to tell him about my idea of listing my research questions and linking them directly to questions or observation categories on my data collection tool. (➡*Tutorial 6*) 'Here, it's easier if I show you,' I said, and quickly drafted out my idea. 'What I'd do is list both my research questions and those contained in the questionnaire and then draw lines to indicate which questions help answer my research questions (see figure on p. 137).'

'That's very good. Where did you get that idea from?'

'It was something that came to me when I was reviewing our last tutorial.'

'Well it's a really good idea – which, if used with my boxes (see Handout 6.2), would help align your research focus, research questions and the questions or headings in your data collection methods. Do you mind if I pinch it for my other students?'

'No, not at all,' I said, feeling pleased. Clearly it's not just the experts who can come up with a good idea.

Piloting my questionnaire

'Once you've confirmed that you're collecting the data you need to answer your research questions, what do you need to do with the questionnaire?'

'I've always been told that you must pilot a questionnaire,' I said.

'Correct. And who should you pilot the questionnaire with?'

'Well, I'd give it to a colleague first and ask them to check it for use of English and clarity of meaning. That way I could pick up on any questions that were ambiguous. Then I'd amend it in the light of any feedback that they gave me and only then would I pilot it with a representative sample of my intended participants.'

'I can see that you've done this before. I like the idea of getting the questionnaire checked by a colleague, and don't forget that you can also run it past your hard-working supervisor. I would also ask the colleague to look out for any compound questions that you might have missed. These can be difficult to spot. I remember asking the question "on a scale of 1 to 5, with 5 being excellent, how would you describe management and leadership in the school?" The problem was that, while management and leadership are linked concepts, they are not the same, and you could have good management but poor leadership or vice versa. So, I was unable to use the answers to that question in my report because I didn't know if the respondents were grading the school's management or leadership. But why give it to participants if a colleague has checked it?'

'Just because a colleague understands your questionnaire doesn't mean that a child or parent will. Teachers use a lot of jargon and, although my colleague would understand it, my intended participants might not. I also need to check how long it takes a participant to complete the questionnaire.'

'Very good. Questionnaires are hard to design. They take a lot more time to develop than a set of interview questions. But once completed they are comparatively easy to analyse.'

Analysing my questionnaire

'Do I need a computer package to analyse my questionnaire?'

'The value of most packages on offer is that they can perform various statistical calculations for you. However, the difficulty is usually choosing which statistical test to use. Sometimes samples in small-scale projects are so small that statistically significant results are unobtainable. The data from most small-scale research projects can be analysed manually or by using Excel. Of course, if you intend to use questionnaires frequently, you might consider looking at questionnaire design and analysis software such as SNAP or SurveyMonkey. Both are available in our IT suites and most colleges and universities offer access to similar packages. If you're considering using them in the future, you should Google them for more information. We'll be talking more about analysis of data in a couple of weeks' time. (➡ *Tutorial 9*) So, all I'll say now is that as you design your questionnaire give some thought to how you will analyse your results. Many students only think about this after they have collected their data and this can cause problems.'

How many questionnaires do I need and how can I improve return rates?

'OK,' I said. As Richard shifted in his chair I piped up with a question that had been on my mind. 'I know what you're going to say but I'm going to ask it anyway. How many questionnaires do I need returned for my project?'

'You know me so well,' he said, smiling. 'As you rightly guessed, you need as many questionnaires returned as are required to answer your research questions. What you really need is enough relevant and interesting data to fill your findings section. What is certain is that if you send the questionnaire by post or email you won't get a 100 per cent response. Typically the response rate on postal questionnaires is around 22 per cent. Obviously this is higher when you send the questionnaire to people you know. The best return rate is when you have a captive audience and participants complete the questionnaire while you are present – for example, when you collect data from your own class. However, we come back to the question of informed consent. (➡ *Tutorial 4*) You shouldn't use your position to force anyone to fill in a questionnaire.'

'How can I improve the response rate from my colleagues?'

'We spoke last time about the importance of explaining to people the purpose of your research and the basis upon which they take part in it. So, before you send your questionnaire to colleagues, have a chat with them about your research and ask them if they are willing to fill in your questionnaire. If you're sending your questionnaire to strangers, by post or email, then the importance of this communication increases significantly. A well-written request will increase the return rate. What do you think should go in such a letter?'

Unless it was a trick question the answer seemed obvious. 'It would cover the same issues as the letter or email you send to people you're going to interview or observe. So it would talk about anonymity, the fact that completion of the questionnaire isn't compulsory and how participants can get a copy of the final report. All those sort of things.'

'Good. You've clearly got the right idea. If you want to see an example of the kind of letter that can accompany a questionnaire go to my website **www.routledge. com/9780273774792.** You should also enclose a stamped addressed envelope if it's a postal questionnaire. To improve response rates you can think about sending a polite follow-up letter or email to non-responders. But don't deluge the person with reminders; it will only irritate them. One reminder is sufficient. And don't, whatever you do, design a questionnaire that takes ages to complete.'

Working at Master's level: Using documents and literature as data

'So what about studying at Master's level? I suppose everything you said about making sure that I discuss the strengths and weakness of my data collection methods in the context of my own research applies here as well.' (➡ *Tutorials 5 and 6*)

'Indeed it does. But writing at Master's level also opens up opportunities that are limited to you at undergraduate level. For example, a typical Dissertation at Master's level is about 15,000 words. That makes it much more feasible for you to base your research on just literature and documents. I've seen some very good work where students simply explored a subject using literature and other documentary evidence.'

'What sort of assignments?'

'Students have looked at models of reflection, assessment, feedback, learning styles and even teaching methods. What they have tried to do is summarise the latest thinking on the issue and using reflection and critical evaluation try to identify where they stand on the issue in question. When it works it's great, but if you have difficulty critically evaluating literature it's not something you should try.'

'Wouldn't it be more interesting to undertake some empirical research and collect some data.'

'Perhaps. But often these students have problems concerning access or they're thinking of doing an EdD or PhD and want to use the dissertation as a way of identifying current thought in the field they are interested in.'

'That approach isn't going to be suitable for my PGCE project.'

'No, but it's something to keep in mind if you ever want to do a Master's or Doctorate.'

Working at Master's level: Using questionnaires

'What about questionnaires at Master's level? What do I need to do . . . ?'

'At undergraduate level you might be able to do a small project just using a questionnaire. Why do you think you wouldn't get away with that at Master's level?'

I surprised myself by answering almost immediately. 'The level of detail that you can get from a questionnaire is limited. The data collected would be largely superficial and you said that at Master's level depth was more important than breadth.'

'That's true. It's also the case that you are expected to triangulate your findings at Master's level and, while you could use stratified triangulation, your results would be more secure if you used methods triangulation. (➡ *Tutorial 4*)

Sam's reflection

1 December

This was a short tutorial. Why Richard didn't tag it on to the end of last week's session I don't know. Maybe he thought it was too much for me to grasp in one session. Or perhaps he wanted to get off to a match or another salsa lesson. Who knows?

Perhaps because I've used questionnaires before I found the session fairly easy. Or maybe I'm just gaining in confidence. Certainly I feel a lot more confident about my ability to carry out a small-scale piece of research than when I started. I'd be in trouble if I didn't! But I think it's more than that. I think I'm beginning to see that certain principles underpin all research, at all levels, such as clarity of aims, transparency concerning what I have done and how I have done it, criticality and a genuine concern for the well-being of my respondents.

What Richard didn't mention is how questionnaires need to be designed with the needs and abilities of respondents in mind. I know from past experience that you can't give the same questionnaire to young children as you would adults. The questionnaire has to be designed with the participant in mind. That's why I'm going to use Likert and ranking questions. Teachers are used to giving their opinions on a range of issues and they seem to be forever ranking things in order of preference. Or is that just my imagination?

One thing the session has done is confirm that I intend to use questionnaires as my main data collection source. What I now have to decide is: do I send the questionnaires to all the teachers in the school or just those in years 9-10?

Record of tutorial

Student: Sam Sylon   **Date: 29/11/XX**

SUMMARY OF KEY LEARNING POINTS

- Documentation can be used as either literature or data.

- Documentation that contextualises the issues or which is used to explain, explore and challenge findings is likely to be literature.

- Documents that contain information which helps answer the research questions can be used as a source of data.

- Whether official documents are used as literature or a source of data it is necessary to critically evaluate the material: e.g. for what purpose were they written? How was the data collected? Has the data been independently verified?

- Questionnaires must be accompanied by a letter or email explaining the purpose of the research, the respondents' right to refuse to take part in the research and the conditions that will apply should they take part.

- A good questionnaire will be clearly presented, unambiguous and relatively quick to complete (no more than eight minutes). To achieve this, a peer and/ or supervisor should review the questionnaire prior to it being piloted with potential participants.

- A range of different types of questions can be used to collect the data required to answer research questions. (➡ *Handout 7.1*)

- Keep in mind the age, ability and level of understanding of respondents when designing the questionnaire. Try to make them as attractive as possible.

- Consider how you will sample your population and how you will maximise the response rate.

- A research project based on documents and literature is very effective in establishing the current thinking on a wide range of subjects. However, the need to spread your net wide and to critically evaluate your sources means that it is probably more suited to longer Master's level assignments.

- Questionnaires are unlikely to provide the depth of data required for Master's work.
- At Master's level questionnaires are most useful when used in conjunction with interviews or observations.

Agreed action points

Sam will:

- Design a questionnaire suitable for Year 10 teachers.
- Have a colleague review the questionnaire before sending it to me for comment.
- Amend questionnaire in light of comments received and pilot it with one teacher.
- Draft a covering letter to accompany the questionnaire.

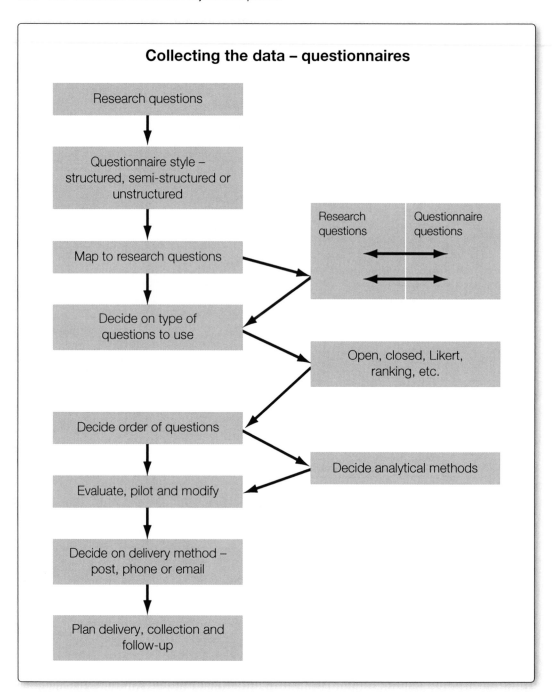

Collecting the data – questionnaires

Handout 7.1

TYPES OF QUESTIONS FOUND IN A QUESTIONNAIRE

Question type	Example
Closed	Please state your: Name Age Gender
Range questions	Please indicate how old you are: 20–29, 30–39, 40–49, 50–59, 60 and over. (*Note: Don't make the following common mistake.* *Please indicate how old you are*: 20–30, 30–40, 40–50, etc.)
Multiple-choice questions	Which of the following statements is untrue? Tick one only: During the 1970s Margaret Thatcher was the Minister for Education. ☐ Margaret Thatcher was forced to resign as Prime Minister when she failed to defeat decisively Michael Heseltine when he stood for leadership of the Conservative Party in 1990. ☐ Tony Blair succeeded Margaret Thatcher as Prime Minister in 1997. ☐
Ranking	Rank the following teaching methods in terms of your personal preference, with one being your favourite. ☐ lecture ☐ group work ☐ pair working ☐ role play ☐ team teaching ☐ discussion ☐ discovery learning ☐ student presentations

➡

Question type	Example
Select	Tick each of the following teaching methods that you use on a regular basis (i.e. once per week). Lecture ☐ group work ☐ pair working ☐ role play ☐ discussion ☐ discovery learning ☐ student presentations ☐
Likert scale	Read the following sentence and circle the statement that best describes your reaction: Ofsted inspections help teachers to improve their professional practice. Agree strongly ☐ agree ☐ neither agree nor disagree ☐ disagree ☐ disagree strongly ☐
Semi-structured	Typically semi-structured questions ask you to write a short comment on your answer to the previous question.
Unstructured	Such questions are rarely used but typically they ask the respondent to write a paragraph in response to the question posed.

ANALYSIS OF QUALITATIVE DATA

Aim of tutorial

To enable you to analyse, evaluate and report qualitative data. A step-by-step approach guides you through the process of comparing and contrasting data, including making links with the theories contained in your literature review.

Areas covered in this tutorial

Sam's reflection

13 December

Tonight is the last session before we break for Christmas. I'll be glad of the rest. It will also give me a chance to catch up on some reading. Now that I have a pretty good idea of research terminology I'm starting to find that I can make more sense of the various books that Richard has recommended. Looking around the library last week I found dozens of books on research. I wonder what sort of sad individual spends a year writing a book on research methodology. They really do need to get a life.

Review of tutorial

Richard was tidying his desk when I entered. Old magazines, minutes of meetings and handouts overflowed from the waste bin and formed a large pool of type on the floor.

'It's my annual clear-out,' he said, smiling. 'Once a year I throw out every document that I haven't used in the past 12 months, or which I am unlikely to use in the next year. It has a great liberating effect – especially just before Christmas. Now hang on while I put this lot in the recycle bin.'

I sat down and set up the recorder.

Coding my data using an interview transcript

Richard returned, slightly out of breath. 'Right,' he said, 'Analysis of qualitative data. The seminal book on this is probably Miles and Huberman (1994). There's also a good book by Saldana (2009) on coding data. Both are on the reading list and well worth a look. Remember when I said that interviews, observations and questionnaires all resided on a continuum that ran from structured to unstructured?' (➡ *Tutorials 6 and 7*)

'Yes,' I nodded.

'Well, when it comes to the analysis of qualitative data many of the same principles, processes and procedures apply whether we are looking at data from interviews, observations or questionnaires. So, what we will do is look at the analysis of an interview transcript first and then consider what additional elements come into play when dealing with questionnaires and observation schedules.'

'OK, but remember that I'm most interested in questionnaires.'

'Understood. The first thing you have to do is code the data. Even if you use a computer package you will have to provide a code to identify each element of data that you may wish to comment on. Therefore you have to think about a coding system.'

'I hate codes. I had a summer job in an engineering company and every time I wanted to order a batch of paper I had to fill in a requisition form and supply an accounts code that was designed to be impossible to remember.'

'Well, in that case make sure your coding system is simple and memorable.'

'How?' I asked.

'Let's assume that you interview four teachers about their views on teaching methods. You record the interviews and transcribe them. First step, take a photocopy of transcription one and go through it with a highlighter pen. Highlight any words, ideas, events, issues or comments that you think are significant or interesting. Include any issues that you hadn't previously thought about. Then do the same for transcripts two to four. Leave a gap between each session of analysis and avoid as far as possible any tendency to consciously look for the same issues that you identified previously. And don't ignore the mundane and apparently boring for the sake of the unusual and exciting.'

'But what about the coding?' I asked.

An example of a coding system

'I'm coming to that. Take transcript one. We can call it teacher one or transcript one. Either way, the first part of your code is T1. The second part relates to the page number on the transcript – say, page 2. The third part relates to a theme. Now you're looking at teaching methods in your first research question, so one of your themes could be student-centred methods. So your code reads T1/P2/T1. You write that in the margin next to the paragraph or section in which that theme is discussed.'

'OK, I get it. The code means teacher 1, page 2, and theme 1 student-centred methods.'

'Correct. When you have identified all the broad themes in a transcript go a level lower and identify the different issues that relate to each theme. For example Theme 1 relates to the student-centred teaching methods. Now you have to break that down into a series of issues that identifies each teaching method used and what people say about each method. So you might have Issue 1, strengths of group work; Issue 2, weaknesses of group work; Issue 3, learners' attitudes to group work.'

'So if I was talking about the weakness of group work it would be Issue 2 and my code would be T1/P2/T1/I2.'

'Precisely, and a strength of group work would be T1/P2/T1/I1.'

'But I could make each different teaching method an issue and then have a separate code to identify specific features of that method.'

'Go on.'

'Well, it could be T1/P2/T1/I1/SI2. Which would mean teacher 1, page 2, theme 1 teaching methods, issue 1 group work and sub-issue 2 weaknesses.'

'You could, but it's starting to get a bit complicated. What is essential is that you draw up a coding system that is logical, works for you and which you can explain to the reader. But what is absolutely essential is that you record, and keep safe, the details of your coding system. Don't think that you will remember it. Write down what each element of the code means. There is nothing worse than coding all your data and then when you return to it a week later you can't remember what some of the codes mean.'

'But couldn't you identify all the issues first and then summarise them into themes?'

'Indeed you could. Personally I like to work from the top down; it seems more logical to me, but that's a personal preference. And your suggestion would be inline with a grounded theory approach. (➡ *Tutorial 5*) As I say, what's essential is that the coding system is meaningful to you and that your analysis helps you answer your research questions. It's no use coding items that have no significance in terms of your research questions. Unless it's that rare commodity "valuable unexpected findings". In which case you may want to review your research questions and change them to allow for inclusion in your findings for this gold dust.'

'I can see the point of coding themes and issues, but why bother with teacher and page?'

'You may want to report that Teacher 1 held particular views or you may want to quote what they said.'

'But why the page number?'

'If you quote what they said you will need to provide a reference, e.g. T1/P2 etc.'

'So, that's another reason why I need to include a full transcript of each of my interviews in the appendix. You might want to check that I didn't quote the person out of context.'

'Yes. After you have analysed all four transcripts, take a pair of scissors and cut out each reference and the statement that goes with it. You can then sort the slips of paper that you have into a series of bundles analysed by theme.'

'Right,' I said, anticipating what Richard was about to say. 'What I'll have is the comments of all four teachers on, say, group work in a single bundle and because of the code I will know which teacher said what.'

'Yes, so you can then split the bundles into issues and if only one teacher raised a particular issue you may decide that it is not worth writing about it in your final report. But be careful, remember gold dust. Sometimes the most interesting and novel ideas are only raised by one person!'

'The approach you're suggesting is really only a manual cut and paste job, isn't it?'

'It is, but I only use it as an example because it's the easiest way to explain the principle of coding. As you say you can do the same on any word-processed transcript by using "Comments" to add codes. You can then highlight all the comments made that relate to a particular theme in, say, yellow. This allows you to cut and paste all the yellow comments on to a single document. Then you do the same with the next theme which is coloured blue or whatever.'

'And because I have coded each paragraph I will still know who said what and I can start to sort each colour-coded file into issues.'

'You've got it. Qualitative analysis packages work in a similar fashion. You identify themes and issues, code them and then link files with the same codes together for future use. If you have a lot of data to analyse, a package is ideal, but for a small-scale piece of research the manual or computer-based methods I've described are fine. Saldana (2009) is good on coding.'

Let the participants speak for themselves

'You mentioned using direct quotes from participants: is that normal practice?'

'I think it's good practice. If you can provide a quote from an interviewee it often brings the issue to life. It grounds the discussion in reality. I'm a big fan of using actual quotes or describing actual events that you have observed but you must ensure that . . .'

'You protect the anonymity of the participant at all times.' (➡ *Tutorial 4*) I finished the sentence for him.

'You read my mind!'

Sam's reflection

14 December

Well, so much for coding. I've been dreading it. But from what Richard said it should be fairly straightforward. What I need to do is design a simple coding system that will allow me to trace back where I got my data from and describe the main issues contained within each theme. Sounds easy. We'll see.

I quite like the idea of cutting and pasting my data on the computer. This would be very useful for direct quotes as I could just copy and paste straight from the transcript. I think Richard's a bit of a dinosaur when it comes to IT. I can see lots of possibilities there. I could use 'bookmarks', for example, to mark sections of text that are particularly important. This would be good for quotes too. But there are probably some advantages to using the manual approach. There might be less chance of getting confused and missing an important piece of data.

I was dubious about using quotes from the data I collect – probably because of what Richard said about not using long quotes in the literature review. But of course a quote from my data isn't copying, it's reporting exactly what I found. Hang on; I've just had a ping moment. If my code identifies which participant is speaking, I'll be able to see how many times I have used a quote from a particular person. That way I will know if I've relied too heavily on the views of one or two people and ignored others. That will help me reduce bias. (➡ *Tutorial 4*)

Review of tutorial

When should I analyse my data?

'So when should I start to analyse my data?'

'That's a good question. Most commentators would say that you should start as soon as possible. But I would urge caution. When you complete an interview or observation or get a questionnaire back, do a quick and dirty interim analysis. But don't spend too much time on it.'

'Why not?'

'Human beings have been described as pattern-seeking animals. If you conduct a really detailed analysis of the first document you receive back, you run the risk of identifying certain themes and issues which you then actively look for in later documents and in the process ignore new themes and issues. Effectively, what you may do with premature analysis is close your mind to other possibilities.'

'So, let me see if I've got this right. What you are suggesting is that I do a quick analysis and then when I have all the data in I should sit down and do a fuller analysis.'

'Yes. That way you have a good idea of the issues that are arising and you will be able to see if you are collecting the sort of data you need to answer your research questions . . .'

'... and do something about it if I'm not. While at the same time I avoid the risk of closing my mind to new information.'

'Correct. If you adopt this approach you will reduce the risk of failing to spot interesting data because you are thinking along previously embedded tramlines or because you are dealing with the data in a routine manner. Like a detective seeking an elusive clue you want to be thinking about the data, consciously and subconsciously, over a period of time. Play with the data, take it apart and put it together again. Look for similarities and differences, issues that support or contradict each other and even odd ideas that don't seem to fit. When you have done this you will have started to explore, explain and interpret your data.'

'If I'm going to do that, I can't do it in a single sitting, can I?'

'No. What you are involved in is a process of constant comparison. This is where you constantly review your data and the interpretations you place on them. To do this you need to give yourself adequate time to think about and reflect upon the data you have collected. You might even go and do a little more reading. There really is no single correct way to analyse data. You need to find an approach that is right for you and your data. But the cardinal rule has to be "don't rush it".'

Sam's reflection

16 December

I can't believe that it is only nine days to Christmas. I need to get organised. I'm determined to get some useful work done on my project over the holidays as well as having a good time. I need a timetable. And then I need to stick to it.

The two-stage process that Richard suggested for analysing data seems sound. I'm constantly amazed at how people's first impressions determine what they think about a person, place or thing. Once they've formed an impression it's really hard to get them to change it. So I can see how dangerous it might be to spend too long analysing the first interview schedule or questionnaire.

I'll look at the data as it comes in but I'll also set aside a full week for the final full-blooded analysis. I'll complete the analysis in three sessions but spread them out over the full week. That should give me time to reflect upon the data and try to identify any possible alternative interpretations.

Review of tutorial

Analysing questionnaires and observations

'OK, now we need to look at questionnaires and observations . . .' (➡ *Tutorials 6 and 7*)

For some reason I decided to pre-empt what Richard had to say. Maybe it was because I was starting to feel confident about research theory or because I understood how his mind worked. 'Let me have a go,' I said, surprising myself. 'From what you said about interviews, observations and questionnaires all residing on a single continuum between unstructured and structured, I reckon that a similar relationship must exist when it comes to looking at analysis of data.'

'Go on,' he said, leaning forward with interest.

'OK,' I said, taking a deep breath. 'Let's start with questionnaires. If I have a structured questionnaire, then by default I must have identified in advance the issues that were of interest to me and framed one or more questions about each issue. And if my questionnaire is logically structured, then I will have grouped together questions that explore the same or similar issues. Effectively these groupings will be my themes. Therefore I have my issues and themes already.'

'Very good. But what if it's a semi-structured or unstructured questionnaire?'

I was on a roll and replied confidently, 'In the case of an unstructured questionnaire, I'd treat the responses received like the transcript of an interview. I'd highlight and code the issues pretty much as you outlined earlier.'

'And the semi-structured questionnaire?'

'The semi-structured questionnaire would have some structured questions and some unstructured answers written by the participant. So I'd use a combination of the above approaches. Summarising the responses to the structured questions as outlined previously and treating the participants' comments as a series of excerpts from an interview transcript.'

'Excellent. That's exactly the approach I'd use. But what about observation schedules?'

'The same principles apply. The only difference is that where you have a semi-structured observation or an unstructured observation the notes and comments that you will be analysing will be your own rather than the views of the respondent.'

'And what about notes that you have made as a result of participant observations?'

'I'd analyse them just the same as I would an interview transcript.' I paused, a thought floating just outside my consciousness.

'What is it?' asked Richard.

'I was thinking,' I said, uncertainly, 'maybe observation notes are a bit like the notes you take in an interview when you can't record the session, while a reflective diary is more like a full interview transcript. Does that make sense?'

'It does indeed. I wouldn't say that it is a perfect match but it's not a bad analogy. Anything that helps you make sense of what you're doing is useful.'

Sam's reflection

16 December

Heck that felt good! I sounded really confident about what I was saying. Perhaps it is as Richard keeps saying, research is a simple process provided you can cut through the jargon and detail and look at the fundamental principles that underpin it. Once you clearly understand them it's possible to think your way through a project. It really isn't rocket science. Which reminds me. Last week when I used that expression one of the kids asked me what phrase do rocket scientists use? I suggested, 'It's not brain surgery' There's always one.

Review of tutorial

Presentation of qualitative data

'So have you got any advice on how best to present the data in the final report?'

'Some. As we have previously discussed, what you need to do in the findings is analyse the data that you have collected. Because qualitative data is mainly concerned with words it's usually presented in a discursive manner. Typically you would report or describe the data and then analyse it using the theories in your literature review to explain, explore and challenge what you have found. You can then use your own powers of logic, induction and deduction to dig into the data, while all the time looking for alternative interpretations.'

'But what about diagrams and tables?'

'I was coming to that. There is no reason why you can't use many of the tools that quantitative researchers use to present their data such as bar charts, **histograms** and **pie charts**. We will be looking at these in the next tutorial on quantitative data analysis and there are some simple examples on my website **(www.routledge.com/9780273774792)** on how they can be applied in qualitative research. But for the moment I'd just like to look at how you can use tables to summarise qualitative data.'

'Do you want me to look at the examples on the website before our next meeting?'

'That would be very helpful. But for the moment let's stick with tables. You will need to refer to my handout for today as we go through this. (➡ *Handout 8.1*) 'Suppose you undertake four semi-structured interviews and you want to summarise, compare and contrast the views of the participants. You could produce a table where each participant is given a column and the issues you have identified are written down the side. You then cut and paste what each participant said about the issue into the relevant column. This both summarises and compares and contrasts the responses of the participants using very few words. You can then analyse and comment on the table to your heart's content.'

'Could I use the same approach to summarise the theories or definitions of different writers in my literature review?'

'Absolutely. As I always say, anything that helps you to communicate more clearly with your reader is to be welcomed. Tables are also really useful for summarising data from questionnaires, though a bar chart can be really useful for presenting data from Likert-type questions. Either way it's vital that your presentation is consistent. For example, when describing your results you wouldn't report that 60 per cent of people disagreed or disagreed strongly with Statement 1 while 80 per cent agreed or agreed strongly with Statement 2. Instead you would say either: 60 per cent of people disagreed or disagreed strongly with Statement 1 and 20 per cent disagreed or disagreed strongly with Statement 2, or that 40 per cent of people agreed or agreed strongly with Statement 1 and 80 per cent agreed or agreed strongly with Statement 2. Can you see that I am being consistent in how I present the data?'

'I understand the consistency angle, but why use percentages? Wouldn't it be easier for people to understand if you used actual figures such as 9 out of 10 people agreed or agreed strongly?'

'You might think so. But what if you have 10 questionnaires returned and only 7 people have answered all the questions? That means that some questions may have as few as 7 responses. People would find it difficult to compare 8 out of 10 people agreed or agreed strongly with Statement 1 while 6 out of 7 agreed or agreed strongly with Statement 2. Shown as percentages the figures would become 80 per cent compared to 86 per cent.'

'So, again it is about clarity and consistency.'

'Precisely. The last method of presentation that I'd like to cover is the use of pictures and diagrams. It's true what they say that one picture can be worth a thousand words. So think about how you might use pictures to represent your findings.'

'I'm not sure that my data will lend itself to such an approach.'

'Don't be so sure. Sometimes a picture can capture what people feel better than words. This is just off the top of my head. You could show a classroom with the teacher coloured in according to which teaching methods they used. The size of each coloured area would indicate how often they used a particular teaching method. Similarly, the learners would be colour-coded according to which teaching method they preferred the most. This would provide a powerful image of any mismatch between the teachers' and learners' preferences.'

'But I'd need to provide a key to the picture which explains what it means.'

'You got it.'

'I've not seen that approach used in journals.'

'Maybe not, but give it time. It was only a few years ago that academia dispar-aged the use of storytelling as a form of research. But times are changing.'

'And diagrams?'

'These are common. Just look at any textbook. They are often used to encapsu-late a theory or idea and they are a great way to summarise a lot of information using very few words. The thing to do is be creative. To think about your data in terms of three-dimensional models not just two-dimensional words on a page. But – and this is important – you still have to explain and analyse your data. The picture or diagram by itself is not enough.'

Working at Master's level

'So what about working at Master's level?'

'I'm not going to make it easy for you. We're near the end of the module, so what do you think the differences will be?' Richard asked.

I hate it when he does that. But Richard is a great one for thinking in terms of principles, so I tried to guess what he would say. Finally I said, 'Right at the start you said that Master's work was about depth not breadth. So I'm guessing that I don't need to collect more data. I just need to go deeper into the analysis of the data I've already got.'

Going deeper with my analysis

'Go on.'

'Well I need to go beyond identifying the themes and issues in the data.'

'And how would you do that?'

'I'd look at the issues and see if they could be broken down further.'

'Good, but give me an example.'

'Let's say that one of my issues is that learners don't like role play as a teaching method. I could identify the reasons they don't like it, such as embarrassment, not wanting to look stupid in front of their mates, or feeling that role play is something only primary school kids should do.'

'That's good. Digging deeper into your data is what Master's level work is all about, but you can also look across your data.'

'Meaning?' I asked.

'There's a danger that by splitting your data down into issues you fail to see the linkages that exist between, say, issues. For example, if you were looking at staffs' attitude to management, Issue 6 might be about how they feel undervalued in the workplace and Issue 9 about the use of emails in the organisation. Staff may say very often they are told about changes and developments in the school by email. It would be reasonable for you to draw the conclusion that this was one of the factors that caused staff to feel undervalued even though none had specifically mentioned emails when discussing Issue 6.'

'And I can make those sort of claims?'

'It's a reasonable and logical assumption to make. So yes, you can.'

'Anything else?'

Report data from all sources before analysis

'Let's say that one of your issues is the use of role play. You've collected data on it using interviews and observations. Now some students report the data they got from their interviews and analyse it and only when they have done that do they report and analyse the data from their observations. Can you see how such an approach fails to make the most of the data?'

'Yes, but I'm surprised that anyone would do that,' I said. 'It's obvious that you should report all the data you have on an issue, from all your sources, before you start to analyse it. Otherwise, you'll be presenting a series of partial pictures of what's going on rather than a single detailed picture. Besides, wouldn't such an approach mess up your triangulation? (➡ *Tutorial 4*) I mean one data collection method is meant to either confirm or question the data you obtained from the other collection tool.'

'I couldn't agree more. What I'm saying is that weak undergraduate students can just about get away with reporting data from two or more sources separately, but a student at Master's level would find a big fat comment on their script and at best a weak pass.'

Using mind maps to make connections between different parts of my data

'I've just had a thought,' I said. 'I could use a mind map to trace connections between different issues that arise in my data. The map could either deal with issues from just one data collection source or across different data collection sources. I could also use it to identify contradictions in the data collected.'

'That's a really good idea. Too often the data gets reported in isolation and the interconnections and contradictions between one piece of data and another are not fully explored, if at all. If you can do this then you will definitely be working at Master's level. There's a whole range of books by Tony Buzan on mind maps if you want to brush up your knowledge. Anyway, I think we've done enough for the day. Have a great Christmas and I'll see you in the New Year.'

Sam's reflection

18 December

I'm quite excited about using pictures and diagrams to represent my data. It'll give me a chance to be creative and try something different. But I need to keep it sensible. I don't want to do a Tracey Emin or Damien Hirst on my data. The pictures have to be more than artistic and eye-catching, they have to serve a purpose, which is to make my findings clearer to the reader.

I like the idea of using mind maps to establish connections and contradictions between pieces of data. I'm going to see if I can use them – once I've collected some data!

Right, that's me finished until 27 December – time to relax and enjoy life.

Record of tutorial

Student: Sam Sylon   **Date: 18/12/XX**

SUMMARY OF KEY LEARNING POINTS

- Whether you use a computer package or a pen and paper you will have to devise a coding system.

- The coding system should enable you to trace where a piece of data came from and analyse it to at least two levels, e.g. theme and issue. It is essential that you keep a record of your coding system and that you update it as the system develops and expands.

- It is now normal to include completed copies of your data collection tool as an appendix. You should also keep all material (tapes, transcripts, observation schedules, completed questionnaires) until after your work has been marked. They should then be destroyed. This protects you against charges of plagarism.

- Once the data have been coded, sort the material by theme and issue. This can be done manually using a hard copy or by computer using cut and paste. The process for both is essentially the same.

- In addition to reporting your findings, use selected extracts from your data to bring your study to life, e.g. actual quotes from interviews or questionnaires.

- Analysis of data should never become a mechanical task. Carry out a 'quick and dirty' analysis soon after collection of the data but leave the main analysis until you have completed your data collection.

- Undertake the final analysis of data over a period of time and definitely not at one marathon session. Give yourself time to think and reflect on the data. Write notes on what you have found and constantly refer back to your literature.

- A well-designed questionnaire will have sections that could be described as 'themes' and individual questions that relate to specific issues. Where a participant has been asked to add a comment to a question, these can be treated as notes from an interview for the purpose of analysis.

- A well-designed structured observation schedule will have sections that could be described as 'themes' and individual headings that relate to specific issues. Where a semi-structured or unstructured approach has been adopted, the observation notes may be treated as notes from an interview for the purpose of analysis.

- Qualitative data are normally presented in a discursive format. The researcher reports the findings before analysing the data using the ideas and theories contained in their literature review and their own understanding of the issues and powers of deduction and induction.

- You should seek to add impact to your presentation by considering the use of tables, diagrams and pictures.

- Working at Master's level involves delving deeper into your data.

- You should report all the data you have on an issue, from whatever source, before you start to analyse it.

- Use mind maps to identify both connections and contradictions that exist within the data you have collected.

- Everyone in the end has to devise their own way of analysing their data. What works for one person won't work for the next. So be prepared to try different approaches and change tack if one approach doesn't work for you.

Agreed action points

Sam will:

- **Produce a short document describing how and when the analysis of data will be undertaken.**

- **Design a simple data coding system.**

- **Consider to what extent tables, diagrams and pictures might be used in the final report to enhance clarity and understanding of the findings.**

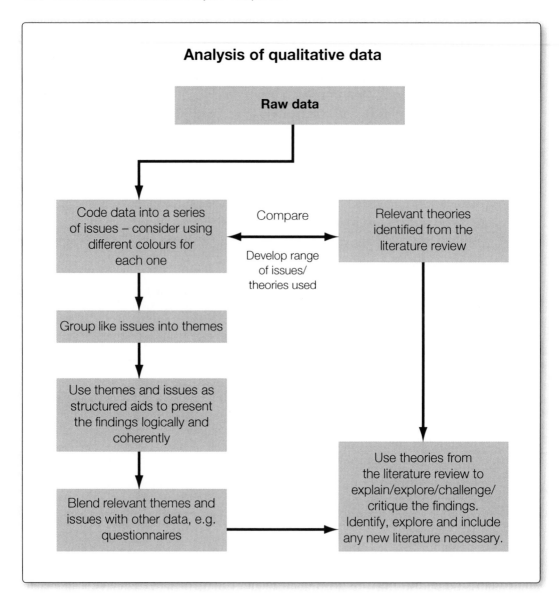

Analysis of qualitative data

Raw data

Code data into a series of issues – consider using different colours for each one

Compare

Develop range of issues/ theories used

Relevant theories identified from the literature review

Group like issues into themes

Use themes and issues as structured aids to present the findings logically and coherently

Blend relevant themes and issues with other data, e.g. questionnaires

Use theories from the literature review to explain/explore/challenge/ critique the findings. Identify, explore and include any new literature necessary.

Handout 8.1

USE OF TABLES TO SUMMARISE AND PRESENT QUALITATIVE DATA

Table 1 – Summarising selected quotes from interview schedule				
Question	Teacher 1	Teacher 2	Head of year	Head-teacher
How would you describe the style of management within the school?	At times I think it is quite relaxed but at inspection it can be very controlling.	I think that by and large it is very autocratic. Only the views of certain people are taken into account.	I find that it is a nice balance between task and concern for the person. Much better than my last school.	I like to think that we are a team and that there are no real chiefs just a lot of hard-working professionals who each contribute at the appropriate time.
Where do you think the power lies in the school?	With the senior management team.	With the head, what she says goes.	With the head and senior management team but they do listen to the staff.	In the main with the staff. We seldom do anything without asking for their views first. Of course sometimes SMT has to take unpopular decisions.

➡

Table 2 – Summarising responses to Likert Questionnaire

Response to the question, I think that:	% that agree or agree strongly with the statement
Senior management team take the views of staff into account when making their decisions.	60
The head-teacher is able to impose her views on the senior management team.	50
The head-teacher is able to impose her views on the governors.	80
The head-teacher is approachable and willing to listen to my views.	70

Table 3 – Summary of 'impressions' gained from participants on key issues by position in hierarchy

Position	Concern for task	Concern for person	Trust in staff	Level of control exercised over staff
Head	High	High	High	Medium
SMT member	High	Medium	High	Medium
Head of year	High	Medium/low	Low	High
Teacher	High	Low	Low/very low	Very high
Note: Having presented your data and discussed the issues fully, it may be possible to summarise a complex argument/situation in a simplified figure. Table 3 is such a simplification. In this case it appears that, the further down the hierarchy teachers are, the more likely it is that they think management is more concerned with 'getting the job done' than the well-being of staff.				

Handout 8.2

Using the terms 'trust' and 'respect' (see Figure 8.1) show how staff think management perceive them as individuals.

Key to figure:

Controlled = Staff who are trusted because they do not rock the boat but are not necessarily respected by management.

Colleague = Staff who are both respected and trusted by the management because their views and beliefs coincide with those of SMT.

Conspirator = Staff who are respected for their experience or academic standing but not trusted because they have a different ideology or vision for education to that of management.

Combatant = Staff who are at war with school management, sometimes for personal reasons, who are neither respected nor trusted.

Figure 8.1 – How staff perceive their relationship with management

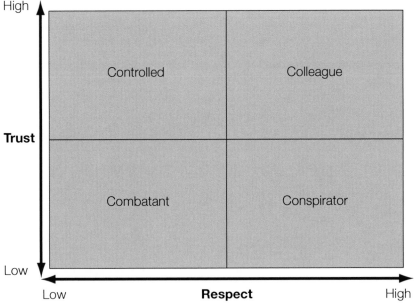

ANALYSIS OF QUANTITATIVE DATA

Aim of tutorial

To enable you to analyse, evaluate and report quantitative data. A range of approaches to analysing and presenting quantitative data is presented and explained. It is suggested that you skim-read this tutorial and then study the examples given at the end of the tutorial and on the website **www.routledge. com/9780273774792** before reading the tutorial again more carefully.

Areas covered in this tutorial

Sam's reflection

2 January

A new year and what am I thinking about? New Year's resolutions, holidays, what major changes the year will bring for me? No, I'm thinking I need to send Richard some examples of data for the next session as we're going to talk about quantitative methods. For some reason he's asked me to send him some test score data although it has nothing to do with my research. I bet he will tell me it's about using a wide range of research tools. At this stage of the course I'd be happy just to use the ones I need to pass the assignment!

I remember that there's a continuum between quantitative and qualitative analysis (➡ *Tutorial 4*), so I must ask about my data and check my understanding about where it comes on that scale. Since much of it's based on people's opinions, I need to be careful not to make claims I can't support. I'm particularly interested in how to present my data in an understandable format. So often I see charts that I don't understand and the message just isn't clear. I'll send Richard some data from my questionnaires and observations a few days before the session. I also have some figures from a government department website that I could do with analysing.

Review of tutorial

'Thanks for the data, Sam; it really does help to have something before the session. It means I can have a good look at it beforehand.'

'I hope you're impressed; I actually remembered this time!'

'It wouldn't have anything to do with the fact that this session is about quantitative analysis, would it? People are terrified of working with a few numbers, but in many ways it's easier to deal with numbers than the feeling, attitudes and beliefs that are a part of the messy reality that is a part of life and the life blood of quantitative research. Learn how to use the basic tools of quantitative analysis and you are away. I'm going to keep it simple but if you get the bug all the highly recommended books cover quantitative analysis and Silverman (2010) deals with the issues in a very clear way.'

Quantitative data analysis starts when you design your data gathering tool

'Can you remember what I said about the first step in data analysis?' Richard asked.

'You said that it begins with the design of the data-gathering instruments. I remember that you often get asked to analyse data and that it's difficult to do a good job when this hasn't been considered at the planning stage.'

'Absolutely. It's like designing a car without any idea of how it will be used.'

'And by the time the customer gets it it's too late.'

'True, though it's not quite as disastrous as that. Can you remember how you would deal with this potential problem?'

'I thought beforehand about the value of being able to make quantitative statements about my data when it's based on attitudes and opinions. Where I thought that it would be useful to gauge the strength of opinion, I included a Likert scale to give me some opportunity to make some semi-quantitative statements. (➡ *Tutorial 7)* I felt that this was important. I suppose that if I'd been using observations, I could have included a timeline and a tally of different events by males and females, for example?'

'Good thinking. With the Likert you've provided yourself with the opportunity to include an element of quantitative analysis. You're absolutely right that care is needed when interpreting these types of data. For example, if you collect some **demographic data** on a group's gender or ethnicity, you can express the different groups as a percentage and be very sure that the number you have is representative of your sample and, therefore, you can make confident statements about the data.'

'Because I counted each one and therefore the data will be accurate?'

'Exactly. But in the case of numbers based on attitudes and opinions you can't be so sure. This doesn't mean that it's not worth making quantitative statements, but it does mean that you need to exercise caution when making deductions about them. Like castles built on sand really.'

Sam's reflection

10 January

Why on earth bother with quantitative analysis when there are limits to what I can do with the findings? I suppose that's just my way of trying to avoid it. I liked the 'castles built on sand' analogy. There are some things that I can measure and be sure of, like the ethnicity of the pupils in my class, but people's attitudes and opinions are like the sand; they shift all the time. So I might make some quantitative statements, but they would depend on the participants' perceptions of my questions and only hold for those people at one point in time and they wouldn't be generalisable.

Review of tutorial

Types of data and statistics

'Let's talk about types of data now and then we'll talk about probability. There are a few important terms here: namely, primary and secondary data and **continuous data** and **discontinuous data**.'

'We talked about primary and secondary data. Primary is raw data like the number of boys or girls in a class, and secondary is when something has been done to the primary data such as calculating the percentage of boys and girls. I'm not sure about continuous and discontinuous, though.'

'You're right about primary and secondary data. Continuous data is data that can be represented on a number scale, such as your height. Discontinuous doesn't usually involve numbers, but categories like male or female. For example, consider ethnicity, the duration of a lesson, test scores and GCSE grades. Which could be classed as continuous and which discontinuous?'

'Duration of a lesson is continuous. They seem to go on forever sometimes! So are test scores. Grades are continuous because they go in sequence; A, B, C, etc. and ethnicity is discontinuous.'

'Nearly right. GCSE scores are effectively discontinuous because the grades produce separate categories which students fall into rather than numbers. Of course, when I took them they were numbered grades!'

'I suppose you had to use a quill as well?' I replied. Richard screwed up his nose, but before he could respond I said, 'But surely there were also categories because you only had the option of Grade 1, 2, etc?'

'Good point! This is a debatable one. Of course, if you take an average numerical score of all the children in a class, then it's continuous because you wouldn't necessarily end up with whole numbers.'

'Let's leave that one there! What's next?'

'It's worth mentioning **descriptive statistics** or **summary statistics**.'

'Not statistics already?'

'These are very straightforward statistics. The word 'statistics' just means figures, data or information. It doesn't necessarily mean complex calculations. Descriptive or summary statistics just means basic manipulation of primary data to produce percentages or means, for example. In many cases it's sufficient to stop there.'

'So maybe I could get away with descriptive stats for my data?' I said hopefully.

Calculating some basic statistics

'Possibly, but I'd like you to have a go at one or two more methods. You don't need a detailed understanding of the maths. Just use statistical methods as a tool. Excel will do everything that you need. For example, if you have a series of test scores, just put them into Excel and follow the path: Tools>Analysis>Descriptive statistics. Select "Summary statistics". Then select the column or row of numbers and click "OK". You'll get various summary stats such as **mean**, **standard deviation**, **range**, sum, **modal/mode** and **median**. Have a look at the website for more details of this.'

'I remember those terms. But I get them confused, especially the mean and median. Can you just remind me what they mean?'

'Well, the range is straightforward. It's the spread between the highest and lowest number. To calculate it you just subtract the lowest figure from the highest.'

'That simple?'

'I told you stats were easy. The mean is the total of all the scores added together divided by the number of scores.'

'OK. So what's the median and modal?'

'The median is the middle score. To work it out you list every single score in order – even if the same number is repeated several times – then look for the middle one. If there's an even number of scores, then the median is between the numbers either side of the middle two scores. The modal is just the most common score. There's an example on this handout (➡ *Handout 9.1*).'

Sam's reflection

10 January

I imagine that the range would be useful to give me an idea of the spread of my data, to see if there are large differences between the bottom and the top. This might be useful when analysing responses to a Likert-type question to see if opinions are quite similar or very varied. I could compare mean scores to look at the difference between two groups such as males and females. The modal score would tell me the most common number of questions they got right and the median is the middle score. I'm still not clear how these would be used, though.

Review of tutorial

'Can you just clarify why it could be useful to quote a median, rather than a mean?'

'Supposing you had a lot of high scores and a few very low ones. The mean would just tell you the average score, rather than giving an idea of how these were distributed. The middle, or modal, score would be a better indicator of whether they were skewed to one extreme or the other. Have a look at the website for an example of this in practice . . . Now we need to talk about **hypotheses** and variables.'

'Do we have to?'

Hypotheses and variables

'Yes. These are two terms that are at the heart of quantitative analysis. We talked about the nature of quantitative data in Tutorial 4 and I mentioned that hypotheses were a feature of this approach. Remember that they're predictions based on a theory. Hypotheses predict how one variable might change when another changes, and it's an important aspect of this approach that only one variable is changed at a time and the others are controlled.'

'I remember that there are two types of **variable**. One you change and the other you measure.'

'Good. The **independent variable** is the one you change and the **dependent variable** is the one you measure. It's important to bear these two types of variables in mind when you present data, because there are conventions to consider.'

'So, for example, test questions are the independent variable and the scores are the dependent one. My hypothesis could be to predict how test scores would change if I included different questions?' I said.

Presentation of quantitative data

'It certainly could. That brings us to the presentation of data. Tables are an important way of summarising data, but it's difficult to interpret trends from them. Graphs and charts show these trends better, but there are conventions for their use. Charts are usually in the form of bars or columns and they tend to be used for discontinuous data like recording the achievement of different ethnic groups, whereas graphs show continuous data. The convention is that the independent variable goes on the horizontal axis and the dependent one on the vertical axis.'

'So ethnicity would go on the horizontal and the test score on the vertical in the case of the bar chart.'

'Yes, though it's really a column chart if the bars are vertical. It's also worth remembering that the columns are separate too as there's no continuous relationship between the different ethnic groups. They're separate entities.'

'But I've seen charts with the columns together. What's the difference?'

'These are **histograms**, essentially frequency distributions. An example would be plotting the height of pupils in a class. Height is continuous, but it can be represented as categories. For example, 1.4 to 1.5 metres. You would plot the number of pupils in each category and the result would be a bell-shaped graph or distribution. This is usually called a **normal distribution**, though technically the sort of result you get is likely to approximate to a normal distribution as there may be slightly more short pupils than tall ones in a small sample, so the graph wouldn't be symmetrical. We'll come back to this later. How do you think that you would show continuous data?'

'Maybe as a line graph?'

'Usually, yes. In this case you're justified in joining the points because you can often assume a continuous relationship between them. For example, you might record test scores for a pupil at different times and plot his or her score over time. Potentially this enables you to predict intermediate scores, or extrapolate into the future to predict possible future scores. Line graphs can also be used to probe relationships between different variables. This is called a **scatterplot**.'

'How would I use one of those?'

'Supposing you wanted to compare punctuality with distance between the school and home. You would assume that punctuality increases as distance decreases, but you don't know this.'

'So I could record punctuality and look at records to find the distance.'

'You would plot those on separate axes and look at the **correlation** between them. In other words the way in which one variable moves in relation to the other. You may then be able to state whether there's no correlation, a positive correlation – punctuality increases with distance – or a negative correlation in which punctuality decreases with distance. Have a look at this handout for examples of these (➡*Handout 9.2*). Finally, how could you represent percentages of, say, religious groups in a class?'

'I suppose I could use a bar chart with a bar for each group.'

'Well, you could, but there's an alternative. Here's a clue. You would be able to show the proportion of a whole.'

'Oh, you mean a **pie chart**?'

'Correct. Of course, you can get Excel to do all these charts and figures for you. The danger is that you're shown a bewildering number of options. The key is to ensure that you stick to the basic rules relating to axes that we've already discussed and that clarity is the guiding principle. It's too easy to choose a format that's the most attractive when it actually makes the data more difficult to understand.'

Sam's reflection

12 January

So, although there are some rules about variables, axes and types of graph or chart, the key is clarity. The point of presenting data is to make it easier to interpret and I can't let fancy designs get in the way of function. Plotting data can also enable me to get more out of it – for instance, by being able to predict trends in the future by extrapolating. I can see that this is useful for my data, but I could also take data from reports, websites and journals, for example, and perhaps choose to present all or part of it in a different way to support or challenge the argument that I'm making.

Review of tutorial

Provide a title, number and legend for all tables and figures

'It's also vital that you comment on data presented in figures and tables in your text. Don't just assume that the reader understands why it's there, what it shows, or what it means. Take them by the hand and explain the data's purpose, relevance and importance. Which reminds me: what's a figure?'

We were back in Alice in Wonderland territory. (➡ *Tutorial 2*) 'A figure is every-thing that's not a table and includes pictures, charts, graphs and anything else that is diagrammatic. And every figure or table needs a title and a number,' I said, pleased with myself.

'A title certainly, but there's also the legend. The title concisely summarises what the chart shows and it's usually placed at the top, but the legend includes a sentence or two of explanation and it goes underneath with the figure number. Tables are called 'Table 1' and so on, and everything else, including charts and diagrams, is called a figure. In a longer assignment with chapters you can use the chapter number first, so 1.1 would mean Chapter 1, Figure 1 and so on.'

'This is starting to get overly complicated,' I said. 'I mean none of this will actu-ally help me to prove anything.'

'Hang on. Remember what I said at the beginning that you're not really looking to prove anything. (➡ *Tutorial 1*) You're building a picture of a set of circumstances and how they affect human behaviour. It's a great aspiration to want to prove something, but in reality we only produce observations which may be relatable to other circumstances. Communication is really important and good academic writing is about clarifying complex ideas; putting them in a simple way. If you label tables and figures correctly, you help the reader's understanding. Do it wrong and you confuse them. And always remember that, while statistics are helpful, they must be used cautiously and only when they can add to the discussion, partic-ularly when qualitative or semi-qualitative methods are used. The other point is that even when you do use statistics, they don't enable you to prove anything. They just give you a **probability** that what you observe is due to chance, and you still have to make a judgement about how significant this is.'

Using Excel and calculating standard deviation

'I can't believe that I am going to say this but, and it's a big but, if I were undertaking quantitative research, what sorts of other things could Excel do with my data?'

'Well, the first thing you could consider is to get an idea of the spread of your data by calculating the standard deviation of your mean. So let's go back to your test score data. You could get a mean score of say 55 per cent as a result of a set of test scores which ranged either between 40 and 60 per cent or 30 and 70 per cent, for example, and you wouldn't know what the spread was just from the mean. Of course, you can see this by looking at the scores, but it helps to be able to put a number on how spread out the scores are. You can do this in Excel. Just select STDEV from the Insert menu, select your data and click OK. Versions of Excel differ, but the principle will be the same. You can then quote your mean to plus or minus the standard deviation. So, if your standard deviation of the 55 per cent score was 10 per cent, you could say the mean score was 55 per cent plus or minus 10 per cent. The larger the value for the standard deviation, the more spread out your data are.'

'Fine, so why is spread important?'

'Well, in the case of test scores you actually want them to be spread out so that the test is discriminating between different levels of achievement towards your learning objectives. The standard deviation may be helpful here. It can be important to know how variable your data are. Let's say you're measuring percentage attendance every month and you calculate a mean. It helps to know how much it varies over that period. The standard deviation can also help you with graphs where you're plotting means. You can plot each point and then plot plus and minus one standard deviation above and below; this is called an 'error bar'. These can help you to draw a line of best fit through the data. There's an example of a standard deviation calculation on my website (**www.routledge. com/9780273774792**).'

Sam's reflection

12 January

I remember the bell-shaped graph. I thought that I would have to plot one of these every time I want to measure spread, but I've realised that I needn't do this. All I have to do is put the data in and do a standard deviation with Excel. And I can quote the spread around my mean. Maybe this would be useful for attendance data too. I could compare the variability between different classes.

Review of tutorial

Probability and significance

'You mentioned probability earlier. What is it and why is it important?'

'We deal in probability all the time. Some things have a high probability and others a low probability.'

'Like winning the Lottery!'

'Yes. If you buy a ticket on Saturday morning you have more chance of dying before the draw than winning the jackpot that night. But tell me how is probability measured?'

'I know that there's a one in two chance of a coin showing heads or tails.'

'Except on those rare occasions when it lands on its side. So yes, that's one way, but you could also express the same probability of one in two as a percentage or a decimal.'

'So that would be 50 per cent or point five?'

'Absolutely. So probability is the likelihood of something happening. Another important word is **significance**. What do you think this means?'

'A result is significant if it's important in terms of the research question,' I suggested doubtfully.

'It is, yes, but there's a more technical definition involving probability. A difference between two means – for example, the test scores of boys and the test scores of girls – is said to be significant if there's a less than 5 per cent likelihood of it being due to chance alone. Many statistical tests give you a figure for probability. This tells you what the likelihood is of the difference between two means being due purely to chance; in other words, resulting from the random fluctuation of events.'

'So if there's a low probability – say 5 per cent – of it being due to chance, then there's a high probability that it's not due to chance and that the difference is real!' I said.

'Yes, a 95 per cent probability. I'm not sure about the "real" bit though, but certainly some other factor than just chance has produced the difference.'

'Why does it always seem to be 95 per cent?'

'How sure do you need to be? If you were 95 per cent sure that you would win the lottery, wouldn't that be enough? So if you're 95 per cent sure – or there's a 95 per cent probability – that a difference between two means is not just due to chance, then maybe you can make valid statements about the data. In practice, you look at the value for the probability and make a judgement. For example, in drug trials being 95 per cent sure that a drug is safe isn't enough.'

'I'd want to be 100 per cent sure!'

'Well, that's almost impossible to achieve, but maybe 99.9999, et cetera. When we use statistical tests, we're testing our hypothesis. It's worth mentioning here that there are two types of hypotheses. When making predictions, we may predict that one variable has an effect on the other, or that it does not have an effect – for example, that gender either does or does not have an effect on test scores. The former is called an **alternate hypothesis** and the latter a **null hypothesis**. Statistical tests are used to arrive at the probability of a hypothesis being correct and we usually use them to test the null hypothesis.'

'Why's the null hypothesis used for statistical tests, rather than the alternate one? I might think that one variable does have an effect on another, yet I have to say that it doesn't!'

'It's just convention. Either way, the value for probability helps you to confirm or refute whichever hypothesis you choose by giving you a probability that the result is due to chance ...'

'So give me an example of a test that I could use.'

'The **Student's t-test** is a good one for comparing means.'

'An appropriate name!'

'Indeed. The test was developed by William Sealy Gosset for the Guinness company in the early 1900s. "Student" was his pen name.'

'Is this where the null hypothesis comes in?'

'It is. So what would it be if we're comparing boys' and girls' test scores?'

'That there's no significant difference between them?'

'Yes. So we either confirm that null hypothesis if the test shows that there's a greater than 5 per cent probability that the difference between the scores is due to chance alone or refute it if there's less than 5 per cent chance.'

'So how do I calculate it?'

'Our old friend Excel again. Enter your data – say the scores for boys and girls – into two separate columns. Click on an empty cell and insert the t-test function from the Insert menu. Select each column of data in turn in the "array" boxes. Generally choose "two tailed" in the next box and "unequal variance" in the final box. Click "OK" and the probability appears in the cell.'

'Seems straightforward.'

'It is, and there's an example on the website. But as I said, it's what you do with the result that's important. The probability value you get is the probability that the difference you see is due to chance, so the lower the value, the more likely that the scores are really different.'

'And usually I'm looking for a value less than point zero five.'

'Yes, though remember that you can change that number according to how sure you want to be.'

Sam's reflection

13 January

I can't see me using the t-test a lot, but it could be useful for looking at school evaluation data. I could compare different schools' data on such things as achievement and attendance. I could take data from government reports and make comparisons there too. These are examples of where I could make more valid statements, as these are empirical data which are not based on attitudes and opinions. I thought that this 95 per cent probability was fixed for some reason, but I like the idea of being able to make up my own mind. Even a 60 or 70 per cent probability could sometimes be enough.

So, I suppose that I could gather some attendance data and compare the attendance of children who are concerned with their safety with that of those who aren't, according to the questionnaire results. My null hypothesis would be that there's no difference between the attendance of the two groups. If my t-test result gives a probability of less than 5 per cent, then I can reject my null hypothesis and state that there is a difference between the groups. Eureka, I've got it!

Review of tutorial

Analysing Likert-style questionnaires

'As you know I'm going to use Likert-style questions in my questionnaire. You said previously that they are a good example of a semi-quantitative approach. So how would I analyse those results?'

'There are several ways. Because Likert scales are always a response to a statement in terms of agreement or disagreement, you can give each response a number. So "Strongly agree" would be 5 and agree 4 and so on.'

'That would allow me to summarise the strength of opinion for or against a particular statement.'

'Correct. The simplest comparison is to score the number of respondents giving a particular response to a statement. This could then be quoted as a percentage and maybe plotted as a column chart with one column for each response. The pattern for different questions could easily be compared. You could also multiply the number of respondents for each response by the number allocated to it. For example, if you had seven respondents indicating strong agreement, and you had allocated 5 to this category as you suggest, then you would multiply 7 by 5 to give a score of 35.'

'Then if I added up the scores for each category, that would give me a measure of agreement as the stronger the agreement, the higher the score.'

'So how would you show that?'

'I could plot the measure of agreement for each question on a column chart. That would help me compare the questions,' I said.

'Yes. Remember a few weeks ago we talked about organising your questionnaire in such a way that questions to do with the same issues are grouped together under a particular theme. (➡ *Tutorial 7)* This then allows you to compare the level of agreement within each theme.'

'What about reporting the responses in terms of percentages?'

'One problem with using actual figures rather than percentages is that many respondents don't answer all the questions, so you end up with 10/10 people answering question 1, but only 9/10 answering question 2. If you use actual figures the results aren't comparable, but if you use percentages they are. For example, let's assume that everyone strongly agrees with the statements in questions 1 and 2. If you use figures, you have to show how many out of those returning the questionnaire agreed strongly with the statements. That gives you 10/10 and 9/10, which implies that someone disagreed. But if you use percentages, both are 100 per cent agreed strongly, i.e. 9 out of the 9 people who responded to question 2 agreed strongly. Personally I would always report the findings as a percentage of those who agreed or agreed strongly with the statement. But that's just my preference.'

'But we talked about probability and you haven't mentioned how that relates to Likert scales.'

'Why do you think that is?'

'Because they're based on attitudes and opinions, so it's dodgy to make quantitative statements.'

'Correct, but it's worth a go, though. There are still a couple of approaches you can take. We've talked about the t-test, so for a given statement you could record the response for each respondent and calculate a mean by dividing the sum of the scores by the number of participants.'

'And the t-test compares means, so I could compare the mean for pairs of questions – say, question 1 compared with question 2, and this would give me a probability that they're significantly different . . .'

'Yes, you could, but there are other valid tests such as the **Chi squared** which you could use. It's tricky to explain and not commonly used so I've put an example on the website. It could be used to look at a single question to test the probability that the distribution of responses – let's say 10 respondents ticked "strongly disagree", six "agree" and so on – is significantly different from the situation where the number of people indicating each response is the same.'

'If it's the same, then they're not giving a strong opinion either way, so I suppose it could give an idea of how opinionated they are.'

'It could, but we've covered a lot today. Let's look at what you have to do at Master's level.'

Working at Master's level: Analysing quantitative data

'OK. But I bet it means more maths.'

'Even at Master's level you can get away with just descriptive statistics. It's worth bearing in mind though that at this level you're supposed to be able to analyse complex problems with incomplete information.'

'So that would imply that I need to use more complex statistical methods? How else can I demonstrate that?'

'The point is that the problems are complex, but not necessarily the analysis. Remember that clarity is vital and you should be using the analytical approaches that are fit for purpose in terms of showing the relationships between data, which we discussed above.'

'You said that graphs and charts are useful for that.'

'Yes, absolutely, but don't be tempted to make them over complex just because you're working at Master's level. Remember that you're not always justified in using statistical tests based on semi-quantitative data.'

'Castles built on sand again?'

'Absolutely. Think whether the data are based on attitudes and opinions, or whether there is a more robust underpinning. For example, this would often come from the use of assessment data; such as test scores. That said, the vital thing at Master's level is to take a critical approach, which we've talked about throughout this course. Effectively, you could score just as highly by evaluating and justifying the approach taken to analysis as you could by attempting complex – and maybe unfounded – analysis.'

'So why have we looked at stats such as the Student's t-test and Chi squared if I'm unlikely to use them?'

'Again it's about informed choices. However, Master's level work does provide you with the opportunity to demonstrate your understanding of these more complex statistical tests and to apply them where appropriate. Just don't fall into the trap of using them just to show off – especially if you are not sure about them and get them wrong.'

'We're back to my Dad's adage "It's better for people to think you're stupid than open your mouth and confirm their views."'

'Absolutely.'

Sam's reflection

14 January

I'm going to stick to charting Likert results. Maybe the stats are a bridge too far this time. I'll have a look at the example on the website, though.

So, the message here was that it's always worth having a go at quantitative analysis, but if attitudes and opinions are involved I need to be cautious interpreting the results. I can see the difference now between the qualitative and quantitative approaches. They seem so different that it's difficult to imagine that they're on a continuum. It's much clearer to me now why it's so important to consider how data will be analysed as the research instruments are designed, rather than leaving this until I've collected the data when it's too late.

Record of tutorial

Student: Sam Sylon   **Date: 9/1/XX**

SUMMARY OF KEY LEARNING POINTS

- Plan for the analysis as well as the collection of data. This includes qualitative and quantitative approaches.
- Be cautious when using quantitative methods to make statements based on attitudes and opinions.
- Primary data are raw data. This becomes secondary data when it is manipulated – for example, by calculating percentages.
- Continuous data are data represented by a numerical scale such as height. Discontinuous data are categorical such as gender.
- Descriptive or summary statistics involve representing data as means, ranges, modals, medians and percentages.

- Excel or similar spreadsheets can do many straightforward statistical calculations using formats familiar to people with basic IT skills.

- There are two types of variables: independent (the one changed) and dependent (the one measured).

- There are two types of hypotheses: alternate (independent affects dependent variable) and null (independent does not affect the dependent variable).

- Bar charts are used to display discontinuous data unless it's a frequency distribution (histogram) and line graphs are used to display continuous data. Percentages can be displayed using pie charts.

- Everything that is not a table is a figure. Tables and figures need a title and a legend with an identifying number. Always make comments on them in the text.

- Statistics seldom prove anything; they just provide a probability that any difference is not just due to chance.

- Putting a value on the spread of your data can be a useful indicator of variability. Calculating a standard deviation for your mean can achieve this.

- Probability is the likelihood of something happening and it's usually quoted as a decimal or a percentage.

- Differences between data are said to be significant if there's a less than 5 per cent chance that the differences are due to chance alone. This is convention and can be changed according to how sure you want to be.

- Statistical tests are used to provide a probability in order to confirm or refute the null hypothesis.

- The Student's t-test can be used to provide a probability that two means are significantly different.

- Likert scales can be analysed by plotting percentage responses. You can then calculate a mean strength of opinion and compare questions using the t-test and by using Chi squared which compares actual and expected responses.

- For Master's level work don't use complex statistics for the sake of it. Discuss the most appropriate approach with your supervisor and above all be prepared to critically evaluate it.

➡

Agreed action points

Sam will:

- Identify opportunities for collecting numerical data relevant to the research questions.
- Plan for the analysis of these data by considering the use of descriptive statistics, standard deviation and the Student's t-test.
- Consider how the data will be presented and select data for appendices and the main body of the report.
- Practise using Excel to produce appropriate graphs and charts.

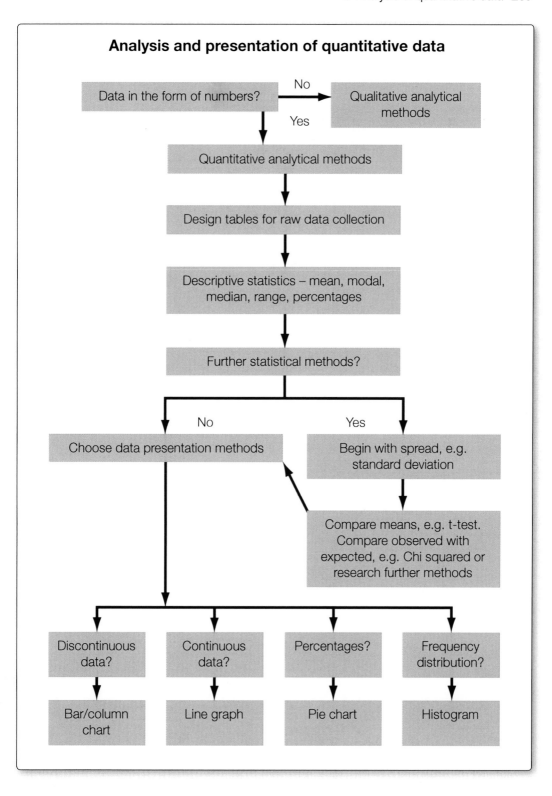

Handout 9.1

DESCRIPTIVE STATISTICS

The simplest statistical test is to calculate a mean or average for a series of numbers such as test scores. Here are some test scores:

Table 1

Pupil	A	B	C	D	E	F	G	H	I	J	K	L	M	N
Score	5	9	12	8	8	6	7	8	7	3	11	2	10	4

- Use Table 1 to calculate the *mean* test result by adding all the scores and dividing by the number of individual scores.

- Determine the *median* or middle test score by ranking them (put them in ascending order).

- Determine the *modal* or most common score.

- Determine the *range* of the scores by subtracting the lowest from the highest.

The answers are:
Mean 7.1
Median 7.5
Modal 8.0
Range 10.0

Handout 9.2

DATA PRESENTATION

Here are a few different types of display device.

Scattergraph

Used to investigate whether there's a relationship between two variables. The points are not initially joined. For example, the relationship between attendance and distance from home to school:

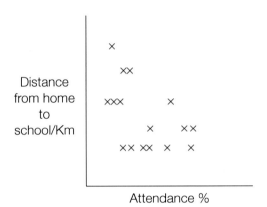

Line graph

These are used to display the expected relationship between two variables, when this relationship is continuous, e.g. the mean assessment score of a group over time. The relationship may be:

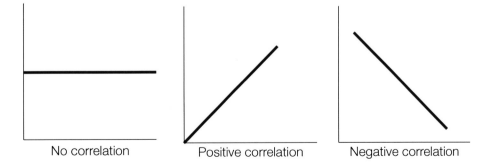

Column or bar chart (there is a difference!)

These are used when the relationship between variables is discontinuous, e.g. the number of pupils in a class of a particular religion. Note that the bars or columns are separated by a space.

Here's an example of a column chart:

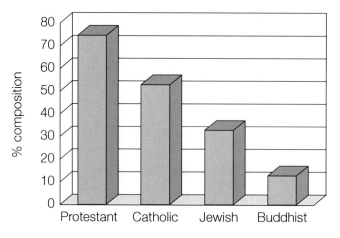

(Adapted from: http://hospiweb.qmuc.ac.uk/imrestxt/quantit/organis.htm)

Histogram

These are designed to show a frequency distribution.

Heights of Black Cherry Trees

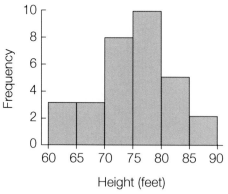

(Obtained from http://en.wikipedia.org/wiki/Histogram)

Pie charts

These are used to display proportions of a whole, usually as percentages:

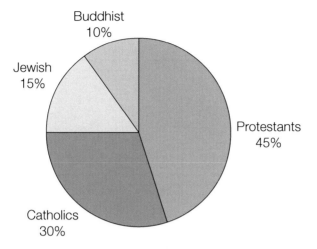

Buddhist
10%

Jewish
15%

Protestants
45%

Catholics
30%

(Adapted from http://hospiweb.qmuc.ac.uk/imrestxt/quantit/organis.htm)

SOME FINAL ADVICE

Aim of tutorial

To help you maximise the mark you achieve by highlighting a number of common errors made by students and suggesting strategies for how to avoid them.

Areas covered in this tutorial

Sam's reflection

21 January

Today is my final research tutorial. I have to admit that I've enjoyed the sessions more than I thought I would. Mind you I still have the hard bit to do. I have to complete the analysis of the data and write up my findings. Thankfully I'll still be able to contact Richard for advice if I run into difficulties and he will be reading my report as I write it.

Richard said that today's session would be fairly short as he just wanted to highlight ways to improve my final submission and minimise any last-minute problems. He also wants to give me the opportunity to ask any questions that I might have. So I had better have a think before the session.

Review of tutorial

When I entered the office Richard was gazing into the distance with that semi-mystical look that supporters of all small teams have when they've beaten one of the big boys. Albion had won 0–1 away at Liverpool. What is it about football that can make a grown man act like a hero-worshipping kid? I handed him the cup of coffee that I'd picked up in the Café Metropolis and sat down.

'The world is a wonderful place today,'

'Yes,' I said, 'it's just a shame you're not marking my project today.'

Simple ways to improve my final research report

He grinned and said, 'OK, let's get down to it. For our final session I just want to give you some pointers on how you might improve your final submission and also provide you with an opportunity to raise any questions that you might have. You should also dip into McGrath and Coles (2011) and McMillan and Weyers (2010) who have pointers on editing and polishing.'

'OK. But didn't we discuss writing the research report in Tutorial 2?'

'Indeed we did. And now would be a good time to revisit your notes from Tutorial 2. The advice on how to structure your assignment will mean a lot more to you now that you have completed the course. However, I want to emphasise a couple of issues and raise some new points. Everything I'm going to say is based on the comments that markers and external examiners have made to me over the years. What's interesting is that the same comments are made year after year about both undergraduate and postgraduate work.'

Richard's final comment was delivered in the sort of voice that said 'but you won't make these mistakes will you?' I picked up my pen and waited to be enlightened.

Richard gave me a copy of a handout and said, 'This contains advice on the common errors to avoid when writing your project and some suggestions on how to improve your work with minimum effort. (➡*Handout 10.1*) I'm not going to go through them all. Rather I'll emphasise the ones that can improve your marks the most.'

I liked the sound of that.

Using a critical friend and student support

'Firstly you need to find a critical friend to read your work prior to submission.'

'But won't you, as my supervisor, be reading the report?'

'I will read and comment on each section. Part of my feedback will be on ways that you can improve what you've written but I won't read the same section two or three times. Otherwise we get into that grey area: whose work is being sub-mitted for final assessment, yours or mine? That's why you need someone else to read the final draft.'

'So what would they be looking for?'

'Good question. But first you need to consider how to select a critical friend. Don't ask your partner or best friend. Neither is likely to be as frank or critical as you need. It is also likely that they will have no understanding of what is required to produce a successful report. I had one overseas student who sent every draft to her brother (who had an MSc) for comment. Needless to say, there was a clash between his opinions as to what was required and mine. It's also a surefire way to end a beautiful relationship.'

As Richard spoke, I had visions of my ex-partner reading my assignment. It was very easy to imagine the rows that would have ensued.

'Instead, see if there is someone on the course whom you respect and get on with and negotiate with them a "buddy relationship" where they read your work and you read theirs. As for what your buddy should look out for, firstly make sure that they have a copy of the assessment criteria. As you know, ours are in the Course Handbook. Secondly, identify your weaknesses. If you know that your use of English is problematic, ask your friend to pay particular attention to the clarity of expression, grammar and syntax. If you tend to be verbose, ask them to highlight any padding, or, if you don't trust your powers of analysis, ask them to concentrate on that.'

'That sounds a bit like peer observations where you identify which elements of the lesson you want your colleague to assess,' I said.

'Exactly! But while we're on this don't forget that you can also enlist the aid of the Student Support Team (SST). We were one of the first universities to have such a team and now most colleges and universities have one. They'll read your report and comment on the structure, how logically organised the material is and your use of English. But because they are a non-specialist staff they won't comment on the content of your work.'

My final edit

Richard took another sip of his coffee before continuing, 'However, you must always remember that whether you use a critical friend or the SST you are ultimately responsible for what you submit. Therefore, I strongly recommend that, when you have completed writing, editing and checking your assignment, you put it in a drawer for a week and forget all about it. Then take it out for one final edit. You'll be amazed at what you find. Along with convoluted and poorly phrased sentences, missing words, underdeveloped ideas and quotes that aren't linked to anything you will discover some really good writing. You will also find clever ideas and good examples of analysis and linking theory to practice which you can expand on further. But you will only spot these if you give yourself time to stand back from the work and review it with fresh eyes.'

Sam's reflection

22 January

I know just who I'm going to ask to be my critical friend. Let's hope that no one else has grabbed her! I should have organised this earlier. I've used buddies in the past to assess my teaching and I know how useful they can be when you get the right one. But I did have that horrible experience with Ben who seemed intent on only pointing out my failures. I can do without that. I doubt that I'll bother with the SST. Based on the comments on previous assignments my use of English and organisational skills are fine.

I do like the idea of putting the assignment in a drawer for a week before I do the final edit. But that means that I have to build this delay into my timetable. If I'm going to do it I probably need to allow about 10 days for it in total.

Review of tutorial

Don't report what writers have said: explain their ideas

'One error that will significantly reduce your mark is if you report what writers have said rather than explain their ideas.'

'Sorry, I don't understand what you mean.'

'I'm not surprised. I always seem to have trouble explaining this problem clearly. Let me give you an example. A student might write: "Charles Handy (1991) in his seminal book *The Gods of Management* describes four organisational cultures. These can be compared with the eight that Morgan (1997) outlines in his book *Images of Organisations*." That statement tells me nothing about the 12 organisational cultures that Handy and Morgan describe. Nor does it allow me to assess the writer's understanding of the theories in question. The information provided could have been taken from the blurb on the back of the book.'

'So what you're saying is that I must demonstrate my familiarity and understanding of the theories and not just report their existence.'

'Precisely. What is required is something like "Handy (1991) suggests that in any organisation there are four types of cultures. These are Club, Role, Task and Individual". You would then define and explain each culture before . . .'

'Doing the same with Morgan and only then compare and contrast the two theories,' I suggested.

Never discuss a theory or a piece of data unless you fully understand it

'Yes, so in effect you're demonstrating your understanding of the writers' theories. Which reminds me, never discuss a theory that you don't fully understand because . . .'

'Because it is better to stay quiet and have people think you are a fool than open your mouth and confirm it,' I suggested.

Richard laughed and asked, 'Who was it that said that?'

'I'm not sure but it was one of my mother's favourite sayings.'

Avoid starting every paragraph with the writer's name

'While we're talking about writers you should avoid starting nearly every paragraph in the Literature Review with a writer's name. For example, you could rewrite the above reference to Handy as follows: "In any organisation there are four types of cultures, but what makes each organisation's culture unique is how these four are mixed. These sub-cultures are Club, Role, Task and Individual. A role culture is one in which ... (Handy 1991)." Can you see that by placing the reference after the explanation you make the material your own while at the same time fully acknowledging where the ideas have come from. Try it on some of the passages in your literature review and you will be amazed at how much more authoritative your prose will sound.'

'OK I'll give it a try,' I said, not at all convinced that it would make much difference.

Structuring a research project and avoiding surprises

'The last point that I would like to raise is the need to produce an assignment that's logically structured. Although you're writing an academic report, you are also telling the story of your research. A good writer will take the reader by the hand and lead them through the story, emphasising what is important, explaining complex issues in simple terms and making it as easy as possible for the reader to understand the arguments. In each chapter you must present your argument in a logical and methodical order with one point or issue leading on to the next.'

'But there are numerous logical ways to present information – for example, chronologically or by theme. How do I know which is the best way?'

'Unfortunately you don't. That judgement is down to you and with experience you'll get better at it. Very often the nature of your study, and the data you have, influences the precise structure. What you must ensure is that if asked you can explain and justify your decision.'

'Anything else?'

'You're not writing a whodunnit. So don't surprise your reader with information or ideas that just appear out of the blue. I remember one PhD student who finished a chapter off by introducing an interesting diagram which summarised the type of employees employed by the firm. It was a good diagram and the idea had come to him as he finished writing. But the diagram just appeared out of the blue and his examiners asked him to revise the chapter and sprinkle it with information that forewarned them of the diagram to come.'

'I would have thought his supervisor would have picked that up.'

'No, he missed it. Both he and the student were too close to the thesis, had read it too many times. As for anything else, I suggest that at the start of each chapter you briefly outline its contents, then discuss the contents and end with a short summary of what the chapter was about and provide a lead into the next chapter.'

'Another case of tell 'em what you're going to say, say it, tell 'em what you said.'

'Yes.'

Sam's reflection

23 January

I rewrote several paragraphs from my draft literature review and put some of the references at the end of sentences. I was amazed at how much difference it made. Suddenly it seemed as if I was a full partner in the ideas discussed, rather than just repeating what the 'master or mistress' had said. I'll definitely use this approach in all my future work.

As for logically structuring my work, I should be OK on that front. Mind you, what's logical to me might not be logical to the marker. I remember a teacher at junior school asking 'when should you cross the road, when the traffic lights are on green or red?' I was the only one in the class who said red. And no matter what she or anyone else said I stuck by my answer. I was only seven but I knew I was right. It was years later before I realised what had caused the confusion. I crossed the road when the red lights stopped the traffic, rather than when pedestrians were given the green light! My logic was impeccable but not everyone understood it. So maybe I'll ask my critical friend to confirm that the work is as logically structured as I think it is.

I like the idea of writing a short introduction and conclusion for each chapter. It means that I can look at the report as five interlinked pieces of work, each complete in its own right, but also forming part of a bigger whole. Besides, although I believe in learner-centred teaching, I definitely subscribe to the teaching model of 'tell 'em what you are going to teach. Tell 'em. Tell 'em what you've told them.' Even so, who'd have thought that it was also the best way to communicate academic work?

What goes in the appendices?

'Have a look at the handout for other issues worth addressing, but for now let's move on to your questions.'

Despite my best efforts I had failed to come up with a long list of questions, and those I had didn't seem particularly important. But, determined to clarify anything I didn't understand, I asked, 'A problem I have is deciding what material goes in the assignment and what goes in the appendix.'

'This causes problems for many students. If the information is essential to your argument then it should go in the text. But where the information is of interest but not essential it can go in the appendices. For example, if you had an organisation chart which you kept referring to in the text then I would include the chart in the text. But if the chart was mentioned just once and was only intended to provide a quick overview of the organisation, I'd be tempted to relegate it to the appendices.'

'But I've read several reports where all the tables and charts are relegated to the appendices. Is that wrong?'

'I'd have to look at the specific report to answer that. But I find it very annoying when reading a report to have to keep turning to the appendices to check on a figure or result that the writer is referring to. So . . .'

'So, make it easy for the reader and put it in the text.'

'Exactly! Markers will look at appendices, but I suspect that some may pay less attention to the appendices than to the main body of the report. If it is important information that you want to highlight, put it in the text.'

'Sometimes I put information in the appendices simply to stay within the word limit.'

'I've done that myself. But that shouldn't be the sole basis for your decision. If it's relevant and important it should be in the main body of the text. However, you can always summarise something in the text and provide the full details in an appendix. This is a good halfway house approach that can be of real help if you are faced with a shortage of words.'

What constitutes sufficient analysis?

'I don't think you can answer this question, but what constitutes "enough analysis"?' (➡ *Tutorials 8 and 9*)

'That is a tough question and it varies depending on the level you are working at. For a first year undergraduate I would be looking for a description of the data and a minimum of one explanation of what it means, with one or two of the more important pieces looked at in more detail. For second- and third-year undergraduates I would expect alternative explanations of the data. These don't have to be diametrically opposite views of the data. They might just look at the data from slightly different angles or use different theories to illuminate the same data. For some pieces of data you may produce two or three interpretations, for others only one. In reality what we are looking for is evidence that you've thought about the data and tried to understand what it might mean in the context of your research project.'

'Does this mean that if you were doing postgraduate work you would need three or four interpretations of the data?'

'Not really. I've tried to provide a simple answer to what is a very complex question. At MA or PhD level it's not so much a question of how many alternative explanations you come up with, although they are useful, but the depth to which you have pursued your analysis. It is possible to follow one line of reasoning or analysis a very long way. But ultimately you are always limited by the number of words at your disposal.'

'OK, so as far as analysis goes I need to avoid providing a purely descriptive report. I need to think about alternative meanings and use the literature review as a source of these.'

'Correct. In the findings section I always worry if I don't see any citations, as it's likely that reference hasn't been made to the literature review. This 'closing the loop' is absolutely vital.'

Writing conclusions

'What about writing conclusions?'

'I use the "rule of three" for the conclusion. Firstly, try to think of the three most significant things that you've learned during your research and consider how you think practice should change as a result. Secondly, remember to identify any weaknesses in your research and how you would change your research approach if you were to repeat the exercise. Thirdly, identify areas for further study.'

'The rule of three,' I mused.

'Yes. Do try to be selective and concentrate the discussion on the most important things. Don't introduce any new ideas or references at this stage.'

Using the marking criteria to check my work

'But how do I know if what I've written is good enough to pass?'

'In terms of the standard of your work you'll have received feedback from me. A good supervisor will discuss the quality of your work and tell you if there is a problem. They may even suggest that you seek help from the Student Support Team. But as you have no problems in terms of the general standard of your work, what you have to ensure is that you meet the assessment criteria. You should be able to check this for yourself prior to submission.'

'How?'

'Come on, you're a teacher. All you have to do is get a copy of the marking criteria which you can find in the "Course Handbook". It is then just a matter of checking that you've addressed each of the criteria in your assignment. You may find it difficult to assess the level at which you've met the criteria but it should be relatively easy to confirm that you've dealt with each criterion. For example, one of the criteria that you have to meet is linking theory to practice. A quick review of your findings will show how often you've used the literature to explain, explore and challenge your findings.'

'Do many students check their work against the criteria?' I asked, sounding defensive.

'No, unfortunately. Yet it's so simple to do. You can use the criteria like a checklist to ensure that you've addressed all the required elements of the assignment.'

'OK,' I said. 'I'll give it a try. My last question is one that's been bugging me for a while. What do I do if the data provide totally unexpected answers? I don't for a moment think it will but . . . !'

'If it does, then you celebrate. Unexpected findings are the sort that researchers die for. Every researcher wants to collect data that confounds expectations. But before you get too excited you need to check that your data collection, analysis and interpretation haven't been corrupted in some way. If you're happy that they have not, you can luxuriate in the knowledge that your personal bias has had limited effect on your data gathering efforts and that what you've found is likely to be of significant interest to you, your participants, your supervisor and perhaps the wider research and professional communities of which you are a part. OK, let's finish by very quickly looking at what you have to do if you do your project at Master's level.'

Working at Master's level

'What I want to emphasise is that everything we've discussed so far is just as relevant to postgraduate students as undergraduates. Indeed, I'd argue that they are even more relevant, because I expect a certain standard of work from postgraduate students and where I might give an undergraduate the benefit of the doubt I will expect postgrads to get such things right.'

'So what specifically are you looking for?'

'Have a look at this checklist. (➡ *Handout 10.2*) These are the sort of things that any marker will be thinking about when they start to mark a project or dissertation. In addition, I'll want to see if the work is at or near publishable standard. Now I don't mean whether it would get published tomorrow in a leading journal. Rather, would it be of interest to a professional audience? If so could it be reworked as the basis for an in-house training seminar, a conference paper or an article to be published in a trade or professional magazine? If it was a very strong piece of work, I'd also ask myself is it worth working with the student to get it published in a peer-reviewed academic journal. Above all I'm looking for a piece of work that demonstrates the student's mastery of the subject that they have researched.'

'Anything else?'

'Get the details right. I want a well-presented, well-written, well-referenced assignment that deals in a mature, considered, critical and impartial way with a subject of professional importance. I don't want generalities. I want a piece of work that is precise and specific. And on that happy note we'll end it for now.'

Sam's reflection

25 January

Appendices still bother me. It's alright saying that if the material is essential it goes in the body of the report. My question is: how do you know what is essential? Thinking about it, I suppose it all comes down to the focus of my research questions and the case that I can make in my own head, and in the report, for inclusion of the data. It's a judgement call and I'm bound to get some of them wrong. Besides, I can ask for feedback from my supervisor and critical friend, so I should be OK. Where I can't make up my mind I could consider providing a summary of the data in the text and refer the reader to the appendices for the full-fat version.

As with the use of appendices, the level of analysis required is a judgement call. Hang on, I've just had a 'ping' moment. Last week I was listening to Carol in the staff room and she said that one way to measure a child's creativity was to ask them to list as many uses as possible for an everyday object, such as a brick. The more uses, the more creative potential the child had. I can see some problems with that theory. But what I could do is look at my key findings and challenge myself to list a minimum of three interpretations for each and then decide which to use in my report. That reminds me of Richard's 'rule of three' for the conclusion. This is going to take some thought.

The more I listen to Richard talk about Master's level work, the more I realise that it's not really about changing what you do at undergraduate level but doing it better. Good undergraduate work should be critical, well written, well referenced, unbiased, logically structured and detailed. The difference is that, if you tick all these boxes at undergraduate level you'll get a good mark, whereas at Master's level it's what's expected.

➡

I can't believe that as a trainee teacher I've not checked my assignments against the marking criteria prior to submission. I've relied too heavily on the assignment briefs given to me by the tutors. That's a mistake I won't make again.

I'll miss my chats with Richard. I've learned a lot about research. But I can't wait to complete my project and get my life back.

Record of tutorial

Student: Sam Sylon   **Date: 21/01/XX**

SUMMARY OF KEY LEARNING POINTS

- Whenever possible ask a critical friend to review your work prior to submission.
- Clearly identify which aspects of your work you want your critical friend to concentrate on.
- Review the range of services offered by the Student Support Team and decide if you wish to avail yourself of any.
- Demonstrate your understanding of any theory that you use.
- Don't use or reference a theory that you don't fully understand.
- Write assertively. Make the material you use your own. Move references from the start to the middle or end of paragraphs.
- Ensure that your work shows consistency and is structured in a logical manner with a beginning, middle and an end.
- Consider carefully what material should be included in the body of the report, included as an appendix or excluded entirely. If the information is central to your argument include it in the text.
- Look for alternative interpretations of the data. Be critical of your own thinking and theories.

- Make sure that you regularly refer to and reference sources from your literature review in your findings section.

- Remember to focus on key issues for the conclusions and recommendations. Follow the rule of three. No new material at this stage.

- Your supervisor will tell you if your work is below the required standard. Respond positively to any advice they give you and ensure that your final assignment addresses all of the required assessment criteria.

- Welcome unexpected findings but check that they have not arisen because of a weakness in your research methodology.

- All of the advice given above applies to both undergraduate and graduate level work.

- A good piece of work at Master's level should have the potential, with suitable amendments/additions, to form the basis for a staff seminar, conference paper, or article in a trade, professional or peer-reviewed magazine/journal.

- Good Master's level work requires accuracy, critical evaluation of ideas, good analysis of data, detail, and precision in terms of both thinking and writing skills.

Agreed action points

Sam will:

- Negotiate with a fellow student to act as each other's critical friend. Brief your friend on the areas of your assignment to which you would like them to pay particular attention.

- Obtain two copies of the assessment criteria, one for your critical friend and one for your own use.

- Check that all aspects of the assessment criteria are covered by the completed assignment prior to submission.

- Use Handout 10.1 as a checklist when carrying out a final edit and polish.

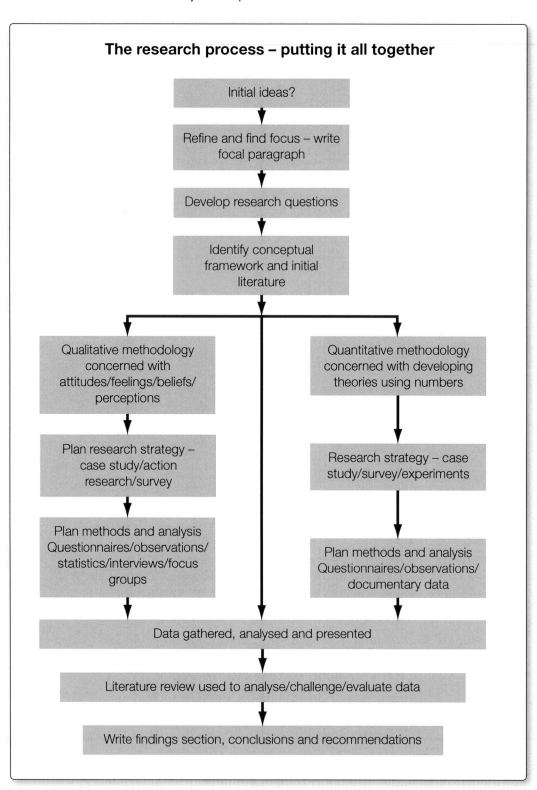

The research process – putting it all together

Initial ideas?

Refine and find focus – write focal paragraph

Develop research questions

Identify conceptual framework and initial literature

Qualitative methodology concerned with attitudes/feelings/beliefs/perceptions

Quantitative methodology concerned with developing theories using numbers

Plan research strategy – case study/action research/survey

Research strategy – case study/survey/experiments

Plan methods and analysis Questionnaires/observations/statistics/interviews/focus groups

Plan methods and analysis Questionnaires/observations/documentary data

Data gathered, analysed and presented

Literature review used to analyse/challenge/evaluate data

Write findings section, conclusions and recommendations

Handout 10.1

CHECKLIST FOR FINAL EDIT OF YOUR RESEARCH REPORT

Your first duty as a writer is to communicate clearly your ideas to the reader. No matter how good or original your ideas are, if your reader cannot understand what you have written they will not be convinced by your arguments. The following is a list of deceptively simple questions which you should keep in mind as you write and edit your research report. By the time you hand in your final report you should be confident that you have addressed all the questions.

- Is the content of each chapter in your report logically structured with one topic leading smoothly onto the next?

- Is the report logically structured? The reader should feel as if they are on a journey of exploration which is clearly signposted and which contains no surprises. This means that the research questions posed should determine which areas of literature are reviewed, the content of the data to be collected and method of collection. The findings should summarise, interrogate, interpret and present accurately the data in the context of the literature and the conclusions should flow naturally from them.

- Unless it is absolutely impossible, word-process your own work. The more you are engaged with your work the better. As you type you will be thinking, analysing and understanding your data. You will also be able to type and retype your work until you are satisfied. If you use a typist you are unlikely to ask them to carry out multiple retypes.

- Does the report contain a balance of description, analysis and critical evaluation or is it primarily descriptive?

- Are there any ideas or issues raised in the report that are inadequately developed? If they are important expand on the issues; if they are unimportant remove them.

- Have you used excessively long quotations in the literature review?

- Have you referenced all materials correctly?

- Have subheadings been used effectively within chapters to emphasise important issues and aid the reader's journey through the text?

➡

- Does each paragraph only discuss one issue or idea?
- Have all tables, figures and appendices been given a number, a title and a legend?
- Are there any incomplete sentences or missing words in the text?
- Does the report contain any sentences that are longer than 20 words? If so is their meaning clear?
- Has each page of the text been numbered?
- Have you used any words, phrases or theories in the report which you don't **fully understand**? If so, double check that your interpretation is correct.
- Has your supervisor read and commented on your draft assignment? If yes, have you implemented the changes that they recommended?
- Has your critical friend read and commented on your final draft?
- Have you carried out a final edit and polish on the report?

Handout 10.2

QUESTIONS A MARKER ASKS THEMSELVES WHEN MARKING AN ASSIGNMENT

- Are all the pages, tables, figures and appendices properly numbered?
- Does every table and figure have a title, number and caption?
- Is the work within the minimum/maximum word limit?
- Is the work logically structured?
- Have the referencing conventions within the text and in the list of references at the end of the piece been accurately and consistently followed?
- Does the title and introduction tell me what the research is about?
- Are the research questions clear?
- Is the literature review critical?
- Does the methodology section describe, explain and justify the research approach adopted?
- Does the methodology identify weaknesses in the approach adopted?
- Do the findings clearly report and analyse the data collected?
- Is the literature reviewed used to analyse, support and challenge the findings?
- Supported by reference to literature and data collected, does the student analyse the findings using their own logic and understanding of events?
- Do the conclusions flow naturally from the findings and identify the most important issues found, areas of weakness in the research and areas for further research?

Glossary of terms

The terms used in research have never been codified. This means that they vary, to some extent, from book to book. This can be confusing. The following glossary defines how each of the listed terms has been used in this book.

abstract A short summary of the research that you have undertaken which appears immediately after the title page.

action research A cyclical process concerned with continuous improvement in which the researcher seeks to improve their professional practice by implementing a series of small interventions and monitoring the impact that each has.

alternate hypothesis A hypothesis which states that the independent variable affects the dependent variable.

analysis The act of breaking down a theory or data into its component parts.

anonymity Ensuring that participants cannot be identified by removing their name or any data that might identify them from a research report (see **Confidentiality**).

audit trail The provision of sufficient information in the final research report for the reader to understand why, how and what the researcher did.

authentic data Naturally arising evidence.

autonomous learner A learner who is capable of undertaking study with minimum guidance from their teacher or supervisor.

baseline data Data collected to inform an action research intervention.

bias The effect of the researcher's or participants' predispositions on findings.

boundary The limits of a particular aspect of a case study.

case study A detailed description and analysis of a bounded instance/phenomenon using multiple data collection methods.

causal relationship An intervention that can be directly linked to a change in behaviour.

chart Usually used to represent discontinuous data – a bar or column chart.

Chi squared Statistical test used to determine the probability that observed results are significantly different from expected results.

conceptual framework The framework that researchers construct in their literature review from the theories of others. This is then used to explain, explore and challenge the data they collect.

confidentiality Not reporting any data or information that a participant has specifically asked you to withhold (see **anonymity**).

continuous data Data that can be represented on a number scale, such as height.

correlation The relationship between the independent and dependent variable. There may be no correlation, a positive or negative correlation.

critical evaluation The process of judging the arguments presented by others and your own ideas. Unwillingness to accept at face value the views of others.

demographics Characteristics of the population such as gender, age and ethnicity.

dependent variable The variable that is measured.

descriptive statistics Basic manipulation of data, e.g. calculation of percentage, mean, mode, median.

discontinuous data Data falling into categories such as gender.

empirical Research based upon the collection of data from participants or experiments.

epistemology The theory of knowledge and what counts as valid knowledge.

ethics The social, moral and professional conventions and beliefs that underpin the basis upon which research should be carried out.

ethnography Research strategy that investigates in great detail the behaviour and culture of a group of people.

evaluation The appraisal given to a theory or interpretation of data prior to making a judgement on its value.

figure Anything that isn't a table, e.g. chart, diagram, picture.

focal paragraph/s A paragraph or more that summarises the aims and approach to be taken in the research project.

focus The precise aspect of any phenomena that you wish to research.

focus group Group of people, usually no more than 8, brought together to discuss a series of questions relating to the research focus.

generalisable The extent to which the findings from a piece of research will be found in all similar situations.

graph Usually used to represent continuous data – a line graph.

grounded theory A research approach involving the development of theory based upon the data collected.

histogram A chart showing a frequency distribution.

hypothesis A prediction and/or supposition.

ibid. Literally 'as above'.

independent variable The variable that is changed.

informed consent The full, free and voluntary consent given by research participants when they agree to take part in research.

insider research Research undertaken by the researcher in their own work or social environment.

instance Term used to describe and help define the boundaries of a case study in terms of people, organisations, events or phenomena.

interpretivist research Term used to describe a range of research approaches that are anti-positivist in nature and deal with people's feelings, attitudes and beliefs.

intervention A change initiated as part of an action research project.

interviews A guided discussion with the intent of obtaining relevant information from the interviewee.

Likert scale Usually a 5-point scale used in questionnaires to evaluate strength of opinion for or against a statement.

mean The sum of the set of numbers divided by the number of numbers in the set.

median The middle number of a set.

mode The most common number in a set.

non-participant observation The observation of an event or process by an individual who takes no part in the proceedings.

normal distribution Data clustered around a mean – a bell-shaped curve.

null hypothesis A hypothesis which states that the independent variable has no effect on the dependent variable.

ontology The study of the nature of existence and the structure of reality.

paradigm A philosophical or theoretical framework. A way of thinking and organising ideas into a coherent pattern.

participant observation The observation of an event or process by someone who is taking part in the process as part of their everyday duties.

peer review A process whereby academics review the work of other academics in the same field of study to determine if it is worthy of publication.

phenomenology An approach to studying the conscious experience of events from the perspective of the individual.

pie chart Circular chart used to show percentages.

plagiarism The act of passing off someone else's work as your own.

population The entire set or group from which the researcher can select.

primary data Raw or unprocessed data.

probability The likelihood of something happening.

professional journals Journals that publish articles of professional interest which are not peer-reviewed.

qualitative research Research that is concerned with the attitudes, beliefs, feelings, interpretations and perceptions of participants and understanding the realities that they inhabit.

quantitative research Research that is concerned with measurement of the phenomena under review and discovery of a single reality.

questionnaires A set of written questions issued to a selected group.

range Lowest number subtracted from the highest number in a set of data.

reflective journal A descriptive and evaluative record of the research progress.

relatable The degree to which aspects of findings in one location may be relevant to other similar situations.

reliability The degree to which the same results would be obtained if the research or experiment were repeated.

research A logical process using data and/or theory to increase the researcher's understanding of the phenomena under investigation.

research focus A statement which specifies clearly which aspects of the phenomena are to be investigated.

research methodology A term used to describe the entire approach adopted by the researcher or just the philosophy that underpins the work, e.g. a quantitative or qualitative methodology.

research questions A series of statements specifying precisely what the researcher hopes to discover more about.

research strategy The structure into which the research methods used fit, e.g. action research, case studies and surveys.

samples That part of the entire population selected to take part in the research.

scatterplot Graph used to determine whether there's a relationship between two variables.

secondary data Processed data such as percentages obtained from raw data or data extracted from previously published material.

seminal works A book or article that continues to be of fundamental importance to a field of study, regardless of its age.

semi-structured interviews A structured conversation where open-ended questions are used to explore the interviewee's opinions on a series of issues, and digression is limited.

significance A difference between two means is said to be significant if there's a less than five per cent, or point zero five, likelihood of it being due to chance alone.

standard deviation A quantitative measure of the variability of data.

Student's t-test Statistical test used to determine the probability that two means are significantly different.

summary statistics (see **descriptive statistics**.)

survey The collection of data from a large number of participants, usually at a single point in time, with the intention of establishing what the current situation is.

synthesis The process of taking the component parts of a theory or data obtained from analysis, and reassembling the parts into something new and/or different.

triangulation The use of two or more methodologies, methods, researchers, categories of respondent, or time periods with the intention of gaining a clear picture of the phenomenon under review.

validity The degree to which the research has measured/explored the phenomena that it set out to study.

variables The component parts that exist and are at play in any social situation or experiment.

Recommended reading and bibliography

No textbook is perfect. No textbook is without some element of bias. Therefore it's important that you use a range of texts when undertaking your research. The following list has been divided into three sections: these are core book, highly recommended and recommended. You should select one or more books from the highly recommended selection to complement *Your Education Research Project Companion* and dip into the recommended texts as required when you wish to explore a specific aspect of research in more detail.

Core text

McGrath, J. and Coles, A. (2013) *Your Education Research Project Companion*. Pearson: London.

Highly recommended texts

You should have regular access to at least one of the following texts. Which one you choose is a matter of taste. All are excellent but they do vary in complexity and scope. You should review all four before making your choice.

Cohen, L., Mannion, L. and Morrison, K. (2011) *Research Methods in Education* (7th edn). Routledge Falmer: London.

Denscombe, M. (2010) *The Good Research Guide* (4th ed). McGraw Hill: Maidenhead.

Newby, P. (2010) *Research Methods for Education*. Longman, Pearson: Harlow.

Wilson, E. (2009) (ed.) *School-based Research: A Guide for Education Students*. Sage: London.

Recommended texts

Texts in this section fall into two categories: either they refer to a specific chapter within a book or they deal with a specific aspect of the research process. Use them and they will add depth to your understanding of the issues.

Barber, R. (2008) *Doing Focus Groups (Qualitative Research Kit)*. Sage: London

Barnett, V. (2002) *Sample Surveying: Methods and Principles*. Hodder/Arnold: London.

Bartlett, D. and Payne, S. (1997) Grounded Theory: Its Basis, Rationale and Procedures, in McKenzie, G., Powell, J. and User, R. (eds) *Understanding Social Research: Perspectives on Methodology and Practice*. Falmer Press: London.

Bryant, A. and Charmaz, K. (2010) *The Sage Handbook of Grounded Theory*. Sage: London.

Bryman, A. (2008) *Social Research Methods*. OUP: Oxford.

Coffield, F., Mosley, D. and Hall, E. (2004) *Report on Learning Styles and Pedagogy in Post-16 Learning: A systematic and critical review*. Learning and Skills Research Centre ISRC: London.

Crotty, M. (1998) *The Foundations of Social Research: Meaning and Perspective in the Research Process*. Sage Publications: London.

Dever, E. (2003) *Using Semi-Structured Interviews in Small Scale Research: A teacher's guide*. The SCRE Centre Glasgow University: Glasgow.

Dever, E. and Munn, P. (2004) *Using Questionnaires in Small Scale Research: A beginners guide*. The SCRE Centre Glasgow University: Glasgow.

Glaser, B. G. and Strauss, A. L. (1967) *Discovery of Grounded Theory: Strategies for qualitative research*. Aldine Transaction: New York.

Hart, C. (1998) *Doing a Literature Review: Releasing the social research imagination*. Sage: London.

Hart, C. (2001) *Doing a Literature Search: A comprehensive guide for the social sciences*. Sage: London.

Hitchcock, G. and Hughes, D. (1995) *Research and the Teacher* (2nd edn). Routledge: London.

Hockey, J. (1993) 'Research Methods – Researching Peers and Familiar Settings'. *Research Papers in Education*, Vol. 8, No. 2, pp. 199–225.

Koshy, V. (2009) *Action Research for Improving Educational Practice: A step by step guide* (2nd edn). Sage: London.

McGrath, J. and Coles, A. (2011) *Your Teacher Training Handbook*. Longman: London.

McMillan, K. and Weyers, J. (2010) *How to Write Dissertation and Project Reports*. Prentice Hall/Pearson: London.

Miles, M. B. and Huberman, A.M. (1994) *Qualitative Data Analysis: An expanded source book* (2nd ed). Sage: London.

Munn, P. and Drever, E. (2007) *Using Questionnaires in Small Scale Research*. SCRE, University of Glasgow: Glasgow.

Munn, P., Harlen, W. and Wake, R. (1997) *A Guide for Beginners on how to Formulate Research Questions*. The SCRE Centre Glasgow University: Glasgow.

Pring, R. (2004) The False Dualism of education research, in *Philosophy of Education*. Continuum: London.

Rea, L. M. and Parker, P.A. (2005) *Designing and Conducting Survey Research: A comprehensive guide* (3rd edn). Jossey Bass: San Francisco.

Robson, C. (2011) *Real World Research*. John Wiley and Sons: Chichester.

Saldana, J. (2009) *The Coding Manual for Qualitative Researchers*. Sage: London.

Simpson, M. and Tuson, J. (2003) *Using Observations in Small Scale Research: A beginners guide*. The SCRE Centre Glasgow University: Glasgow.

Silverman, D. (ed.) (2010) *Qualitative Research*. Sage: London.

Strauss, A.C. and Corbin, J.M. (1990) *Basics of Qualitative Research: Grounded Theory Procedures and Techniques*. Sage: London.

Taber, K. (2009) Building Theory from Data: Grounded theory, in Wilson, E. (ed.) *School-based Research: A Guide for Education Students*. Sage: London.

Thomas, G. (2010) *How to Do your Case Study: A guide for students and researchers*. Sage: London.

Trigg, R. (2001) *Understanding Social Science* (2nd edn). Blackwell: Oxford.

Willis, P. (1981) *Learning to Labour: How working class kids get working class jobs*. Columbia University Press: New York.

Wilson, E. (2009a) Refining the focus for research and formulating a research question, in Wilson, E. (ed.) *School-based Research: A Guide for Education Students*. Sage: London.

Wilson, E. (2009b) Using and reviewing literature, in Wilson, E. (ed.) *School-based Research: A Guide for Education Students*. Sage: London.

Yin, R. K. (2009) *Case Study Research: Design and methods*. Prentice Hall: London.

Useful websites

http://www.bera.ac.uk/guidelines *Revised Ethical Guidelines for Educational Research.*

www.routledge.com/9780273774792

www.oecd.org

www.scholar.google.co.uk

http:// www.routledge.com/9781405835749

http://cw.routledge.com/textbooks/cohen7e/

http://www.education.gov.uk/rsgateway/

http://www.education.gov.uk/researchandstatistics

http://www.socialresearchmethods.net/

http://www.ncrm.ac.uk/

http://www.curee.co.uk/

http://www.nfer.ac.uk/nfer/index.cfm

http://www.bera.ac.uk/

http://www.ccsr.ac.uk/methods/

http://www.qaa.ac.uk

Other texts referred to in tutorials

Aurelius, M. (2004) *Meditations*. Penguin Books: London.

Handy, C. (1991) *Gods of Management*. Century Business: London.

Morgan, G. (1997) *Images of Organisation* (2nd edn). Sage: London.

Index